GUIDANCE FOR THE
PREPARATION OF
PARTICULAR CONDITIONS

FIDIC® Conditions of Contract
for **CONSTRUCTION**

FOR BUILDING AND ENGINEERING WORKS
DESIGNED BY THE EMPLOYER

FORMS OF LETTER OF
TENDER, CONTRACT
AGREEMENT AND
DISPUTE ADJUDICATION
AGREEMENT

First Edition 1999
ISBN 2-88432-022-9

FEDERATION INTERNATIONALE DES INGENIEURS-CONSEILS
INTERNATIONAL FEDERATION OF CONSULTING ENGINEERS
INTERNATIONALE VEREINIGUNG BERATENDER INGENIEURE
FEDERACION INTERNACIONAL DE INGENIEROS CONSULTORES

FIDIC

COPYRIGHT

TERMS AND CONDITIONS

The widespread dissemination, acceptance and use of FIDIC publications and their translations are important means for accomplishing FIDIC's mission and are therefore actively promoted by FIDIC. The sale of FIDIC publications and their translations is an important source of revenue for FIDIC and its Member Associations. It creates resources for providing a wide range of services meeting the business needs of member firms. All steps, starting with the initial drafting of publications, often require considerable effort and expense.

FIDIC regularly updates and reissues publications so that users can profit from the state-of-the-art. By supplying publications, FIDIC does not grant any intellectual property rights. The purchase or supply of a FIDIC publication, including forms for completion by a purchaser or authorised user, does not confer author's rights under any circumstances.

Users rely on the contents of FIDIC publications, especially FIDIC contracts and agreements, for important business transactions. The use of authentic publications is therefore essential for safeguarding their interests. FIDIC discourages modification of its publications, and only in exceptional circumstances will it authorise modification, reproduction or incorporation elsewhere. Permission to quote from, incorporate, reproduce or copy all or part of a FIDIC publication should be addressed to the FIDIC Secretariat, which will decide upon appropriate terms.

A license to prepare a modified or adapted publication will be agreed to under certain conditions. Specifically the modified or adapted publication must be for internal purposes, and not be published or distributed commercially.

In the case of FIDIC contracts and agreements, FIDIC aims to provide balanced and equitable conditions of contract by ensuring the integrity of its publications. A purchaser or authorised user of a FIDIC contract or agreement is thus granted the right to:

- make a single copy of the purchased document, for personal and private use;
- incorporate in other documents (or electronic files) either the original printed document (or electronic file) or pages printed from an electronic file supplied by FIDIC for this purpose;
- draw up and distribute internally and/or among partners clearly identified Particular Conditions or their equivalent using text provided in the FIDIC publication specifically for this purpose;
- reproduce, complete and distribute internally and/or among partners any forms, in both printed and electronic formats, provided for completion by the purchaser or user.

DISCLAIMER

While FIDIC aims to ensure that its publications represent the best in business practice, the Federation accepts or assumes no liability or responsibility for any events or the consequences thereof that derive from the use of its publications. FIDIC publications are provided "as is", without warranty of any kind, either express or implied, including, without limitation, warranties of merchantability, fitness for a particular purpose and non-infringement. FIDIC publications are not exhaustive and are only intended to provide general guidance. They should not be relied upon in a specific situation or issue. Expert legal advice should be obtained whenever appropriate, and particularly before entering into or terminating a contract.

CONTENTS

Acknowledgements

Foreword

General Conditions

Guidance for the Preparation of Particular Conditions

Forms of Letter of Tender, Contract Agreement and
Dispute Adjudication Agreement

ACKNOWLEDGEMENTS

Fédération Internationale des Ingénieurs-Conseils (FIDIC) extends special thanks to the following members of its Update Task Group: Christopher Wade (Group Leader), SWECO-VBB, Sweden; Peter L Booen (Principal Drafter), GIBB Ltd, UK; Hermann Bayerlein, Fichtner, Germany; Christopher R Seppala (Legal Adviser), White & Case, France; and José F Speziale, IATASA, Argentina.

The preparation was carried out under the general direction of the FIDIC Contracts Committee which comprised John B Bowcock, Consulting Engineer, UK (Chairman); Michael Mortimer-Hawkins, SwedPower, Sweden; and Axel-Volkmar Jaeger, Schmidt Reuter Partner, Germany; together with K B (Tony) Norris as Special Adviser.

Drafts were reviewed by many persons and organisations, including those listed below. Their comments were duly studied by the Update Task Group and, where considered appropriate, have influenced the wording of the clauses. Ihab Abu-Zahra, CRC – Hassan Dorra, Egypt; Mushtaq Ahmad, NESPAK, Pakistan; Peter Batty, Post Buckley International, USA; Roeland Bertrams, Clifford Chance, Netherlands; Bosen He, Tianjin University, China; Manfred Breege, Lahmeyer International, Germany; Pablo Bueno, TYPSA, Spain; Nael G Bunni, Consulting Engineer, Ireland; Peter H J Chapman, Engineer & Barrister, UK; Ian Fraser, Beca Carter Hollings & Ferner, New Zealand; Roy Goode, Oxford University, UK; Dan W Graham, Bristows Cooke & Carpmael, UK; Mark Griffiths, Griffiths & Armour, UK; Geoffrey F Hawker, Consulting Engineer, UK; Hesse & Steinberger, VDMA, Germany; Poul E Hvilsted, Elsamprojekt, Denmark; Gordon L Jaynes, Whitman Breed Abbott & Morgan, UK; Tonny Jensen (Chairman of FIDIC Quality Management Committee), COWI, Denmark; David S Khalef, Jordan; Philip Loots & Associates, South Africa; Neil McCole, Merz and McLellan, UK; Matthew Needham-Laing, Victoria Russell & Paul J Taylor, Berrymans Lace Mawer, UK; Brian W Totterdill, Consulting Engineer, UK; David R Wightman & Gerlando Butera, Nabarro Nathanson, UK; the Association of Japanese Consulting Engineers; the Construction Industry Authority of the Philippines; European International Contractors; Organisme de Liaison Industries Métalliques Européennes ("ORGALIME"); the International Association of Dredging Contractors; the International Bar Association; the Asian Development Bank; and the World Bank. Acknowledgement of reviewers does not mean that such persons or organizations approve of the wording of all clauses.

FIDIC wishes to record its appreciation of the time and effort devoted by all the above.

The ultimate decision on the form and content of the document rests with FIDIC.

FOREWORD

The Fédération Internationale des Ingénieurs-Conseils (FIDIC) published, in 1999, First Editions of four new standard forms of contract:

Conditions of Contract for Construction,
> which are recommended for building or engineering works designed by the Employer or by his representative, the Engineer. Under the usual arrangements for this type of contract, the Contractor constructs the works in accordance with a design provided by the Employer. However, the works may include some elements of Contractor-designed civil, mechanical, electrical and/or construction works.

Conditions of Contract for Plant and Design-Build,
> which are recommended for the provision of electrical and/or mechanical plant, and for the design and execution of building or engineering works. Under the usual arrangements for this type of contract, the Contractor designs and provides, in accordance with the Employer's requirements, plant and/or other works; which may include any combination of civil, mechanical, electrical and/or construction works.

Conditions of Contract for EPC/Turnkey Projects,
> which may be suitable for the provision on a turnkey basis of a process or power plant, of a factory or similar facility, or of an infrastructure project or other type of development, where (i) a higher degree of certainty of final price and time is required, and (ii) the Contractor takes total responsibility for the design and execution of the project, with little involvement of the Employer. Under the usual arrangements for turnkey projects, the Contractor carries out all the Engineering, Procurement and Construction (EPC), providing a fully-equipped facility, ready for operation (at the "turn of the key").

Short Form of Contract,
> which is recommended for building or engineering works of relatively small capital value. Depending on the type of work and the circumstances, this form may also be suitable for contracts of greater value, particularly for relatively simple or repetitive work or work of short duration. Under the usual arrangements for this type of contract, the Contractor constructs the works in accordance with a design provided by the Employer or by his representative (if any), but this form may also be suitable for a contract which includes, or wholly comprises, Contractor-designed civil, mechanical, electrical and/or construction works.

The forms are recommended for general use where tenders are invited on an international basis. Modifications may be required in some jurisdictions, particularly if the Conditions are to be used on domestic contracts. FIDIC considers the official and authentic texts to be the versions in the English language.

In the preparation of these Conditions of Contract for Construction, it was recognised that, while there are many sub-clauses which will be generally applicable, there are some sub-clauses which must necessarily vary to take account of the circumstances relevant to the particular contract. The sub-clauses which were considered to be applicable to many (but not all) contracts have been included in the General Conditions, in order to facilitate their incorporation into each contract.

The General Conditions and the Particular Conditions will together comprise the Conditions of Contract governing the rights and obligations of the parties. It will be necessary to prepare the Particular Conditions for each individual contract, and to take account of those sub-clauses in the General Conditions which mention the Particular Conditions.

For this publication, the General Conditions were prepared on the following basis:

(i)   interim and final payments will be determined by measurement, applying the rates and prices in a Bill of Quantities;

(ii)   if the wording in the General Conditions necessitates further data, then (unless it is so descriptive that it would have to be detailed in the Specification) the sub-clause makes reference to this data being contained in the Appendix to Tender, the data either being prescribed by the Employer or being inserted by the Tenderer;

(iii)   where a sub-clause in the General Conditions deals with a matter on which different contract terms are likely to be applicable for different contracts, the principles applied in writing the sub-clause were:

(a)   users would find it more convenient if any provisions which they did not wish to apply could simply be deleted or not invoked, than if additional text had to be written (in the Particular Conditions) because the General Conditions did not cover their requirements; or

(b)   in other cases, where the application of (a) was thought to be inappropriate, the sub-clause contains the provisions which were considered applicable to most contracts.

For example, Sub-Clause 14.2 [*Advance Payment*] is included for convenience, not because of any FIDIC policy in respect of advance payments. This Sub-Clause becomes inapplicable (even if it is not deleted) if it is disregarded by not specifying the amount of the advance. It should therefore be noted that some of the provisions contained in the General Conditions may not be appropriate for an apparently-typical contract.

Further information on these aspects, example wording for other arrangements, and other explanatory material and example wording to assist in the preparation of the Particular Conditions and the other tender documents, are included within this publication as Guidance for the Preparation of the Particular Conditions. Before incorporating any example wording, it must be checked to ensure that it is wholly suitable for the particular circumstances; if not, it must be amended.

Where example wording is amended, and in all cases where other amendments or additions are made, care must be taken to ensure that no ambiguity is created, either with the General Conditions or between the clauses in the Particular Conditions. It is essential that all these drafting tasks, and the entire preparation of the tender documents, are entrusted to personnel with the relevant expertise, including the contractual, technical and procurement aspects.

This publication concludes with example forms for the Letter of Tender, the Appendix to Tender (providing a check-list of the sub-clauses which refer to it), the Contract Agreement, and alternatives for the Dispute Adjudication Agreement. This Dispute Adjudication Agreement provides text for the agreement between the Employer, the Contractor and the person appointed to act either as sole adjudicator or as a member of a three-person dispute adjudication board; and incorporates (by reference) the terms in the Appendix to the General Conditions.

FIDIC intends to publish a guide to the use of its Conditions of Contract for Construction, for Plant and Design-Build, and for EPC/Turnkey Projects. Another relevant FIDIC publication is "Tendering Procedure", which presents a systematic approach to the selection of tenderers and the obtaining and evaluation of tenders.

In order to clarify the sequence of Contract activities, reference may be made to the charts on the next two pages and to the Sub-Clauses listed below (some Sub-Clause numbers are also stated in the charts). The charts are illustrative and must not be taken into consideration in the interpretation of the Conditions of Contract.

1.1.3.1	&	13.7	Base Date
1.1.3.2	&	8.1	Commencement Date
1.1.6.6	&	4.2	Performance Security
1.1.4.7	&	14.3	Interim Payment Certificate
1.1.3.3	&	8.2	Time for Completion (as extended under 8.4)
1.1.3.4	&	9.1	Tests on Completion
1.1.3.5	&	10.1	Taking-Over Certificate
1.1.3.7	&	11.1	Defects Notification Period (as extended under 11.3)
1.1.3.8	&	11.9	Performance Certificate
1.1.4.4	&	14.13	Final Payment Certificate

Issue of Tender Documents	Submission of the Tender	Issue of the Letter of Acceptance	8.1 Commencement Date			10.1 Issue of Taking-Over Certificate	11.9 Issue of the Performance Certificate

Base
Date

8.2 Time for
Completion[1]

Defects
Notification
Period[3]

28d		<28d		Delay attributable to the Contractor[2]	11 Notifying of Defects	<21d

Tender
period

4.2 Issue of
Performance Security

9.1 Tests on
Completion[2]

Remedying
of Defects

4.2 Return of
the Performance
Security

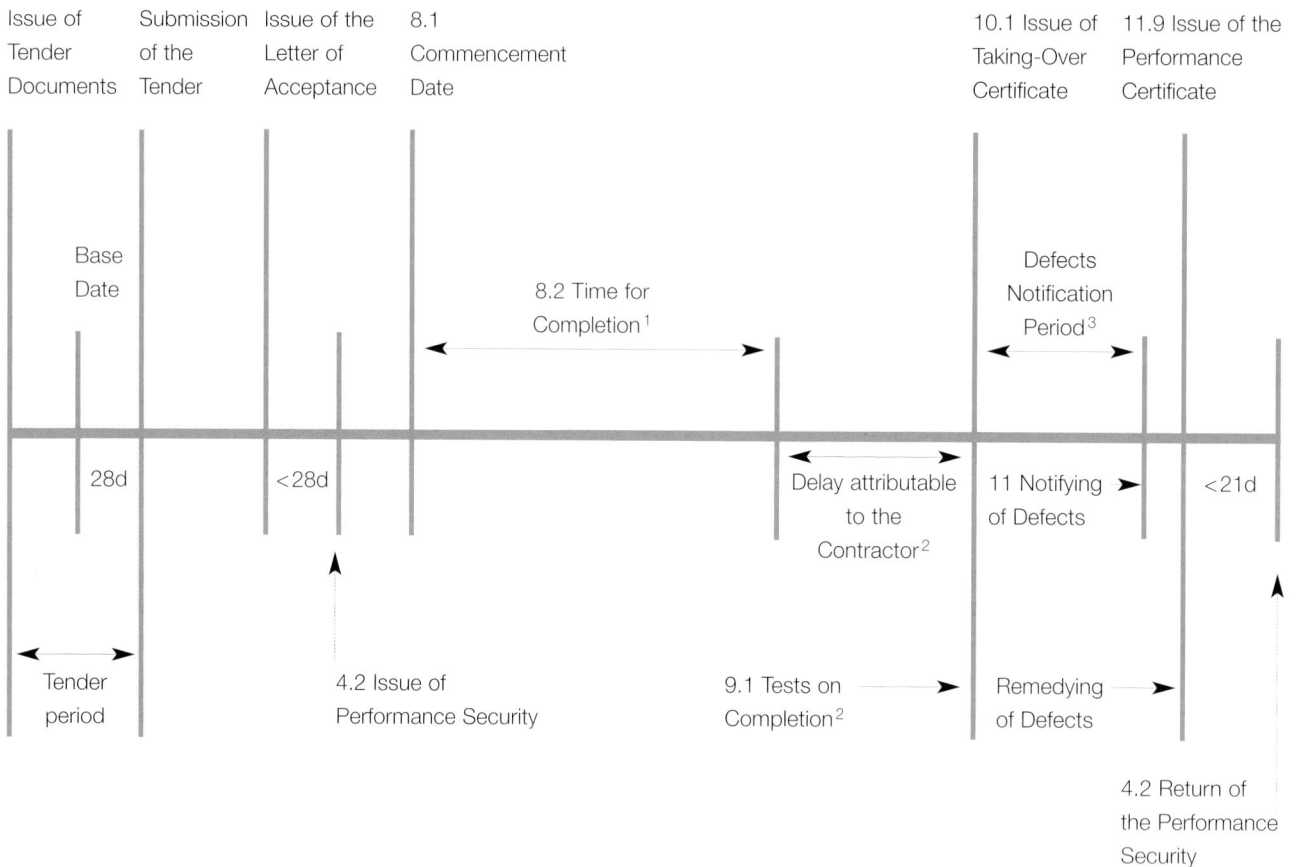

Typical sequence of Principal Events during Contracts for Construction

1. The Time for Completion is to be stated (in the Appendix to Tender) as a number of days, to which is added any extensions of time under Sub-Clause 8.4.
2. In order to indicate the sequence of events, the above diagram is based upon the example of the Contractor failing to comply with Sub-Clause 8.2.
3. The Defects Notification Period is to be stated (in the Appendix to Tender) as a number of days, to which is added any extensions under Sub-Clause 11.3

14.3 Contractor submits Statement to the Engineer

14.6 Engineer issues Interim Payment Certificate

14.7 Employer makes the payment to the Contractor

Each of the monthly (or otherwise) interim payments

<56d

<28d

The final payment

Engineer verifies the statement, Contractor submits information

<28d

<56d

14.11 Contractor submits draft final statement to the Engineer

14.11 Contractor submits Final Statement and the 14.12 discharge

14.13 Engineer issues Final Payment Certificate

14.7 Employer makes payment

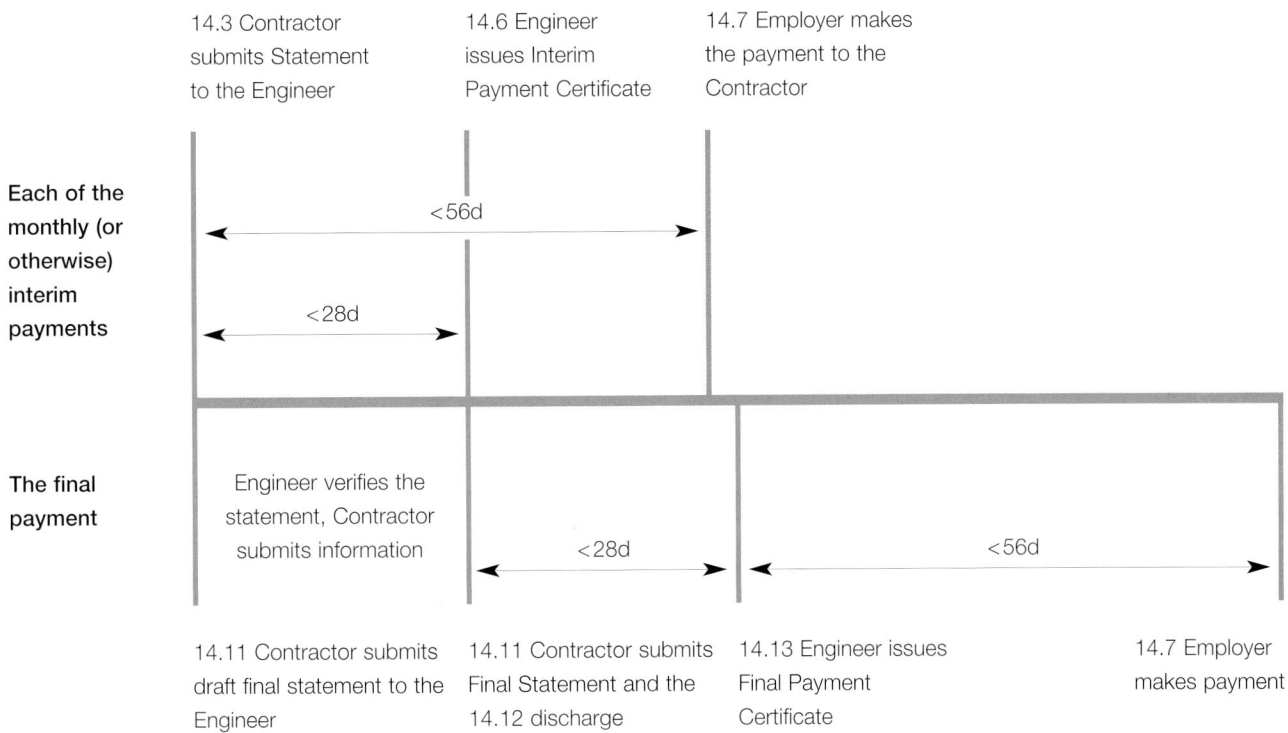

Typical sequence of Payment Events envisaged in Clause 14

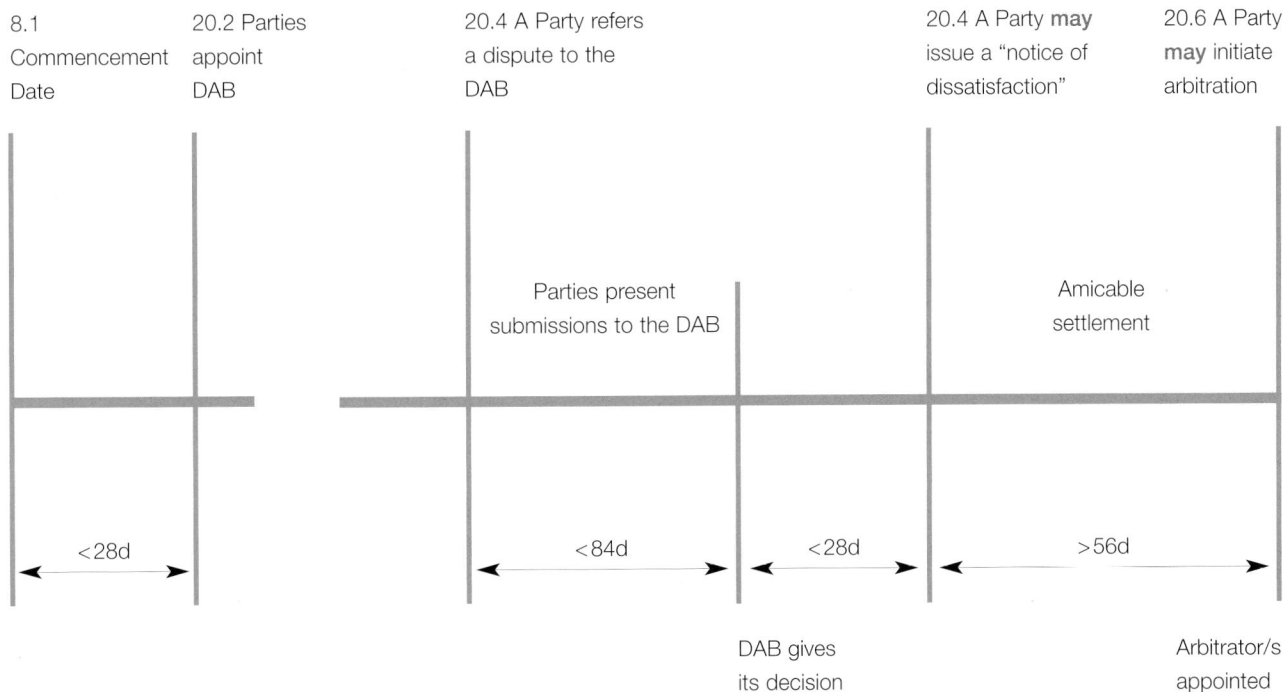

8.1 Commencement Date

20.2 Parties appoint DAB

20.4 A Party refers a dispute to the DAB

20.4 A Party **may** issue a "notice of dissatisfaction"

20.6 A Party **may** initiate arbitration

Parties present submissions to the DAB

Amicable settlement

<28d

<84d

<28d

>56d

DAB gives its decision

Arbitrator/s appointed

Typical sequence of Dispute Events envisaged in Clause 20

GENERAL CONDITIONS

GUIDANCE FOR THE
PREPARATION OF
PARTICULAR CONDITIONS

FORMS OF LETTER OF
TENDER, CONTRACT
AGREEMENT AND
DISPUTE ADJUDICATION
AGREEMENT

FIDIC® Conditions of Contract
for CONSTRUCTION

FOR BUILDING AND ENGINEERING WORKS DESIGNED BY THE EMPLOYER

General Conditions

FEDERATION INTERNATIONALE DES INGENIEURS-CONSEILS
INTERNATIONAL FEDERATION OF CONSULTING ENGINEERS
INTERNATIONALE VEREINIGUNG BERATENDER INGENIEURE
FEDERACION INTERNACIONAL DE INGENIEROS CONSULTORES

General Conditions

CONTENTS

Definitions listed alphabetically

General Conditions

General Provisions

1.1
Definitions

In the Conditions of Contract ("these Conditions"), which include Particular Conditions and these General Conditions, the following words and expressions shall have the meanings stated. Words indicating persons or parties include corporations and other legal entities, except where the context requires otherwise.

1.1.1
The Contract

1.1.1.1   "**Contract**" means the Contract Agreement, the Letter of Acceptance, the Letter of Tender, these Conditions, the Specification, the Drawings, the Schedules, and the further documents (if any) which are listed in the Contract Agreement or in the Letter of Acceptance.

1.1.1.2   "**Contract Agreement**" means the contract agreement (if any) referred to in Sub-Clause 1.6 [*Contract Agreement*].

1.1.1.3   "**Letter of Acceptance**" means the letter of formal acceptance, signed by the Employer, of the Letter of Tender, including any annexed memoranda comprising agreements between and signed by both Parties. If there is no such letter of acceptance, the expression "Letter of Acceptance" means the Contract Agreement and the date of issuing or receiving the Letter of Acceptance means the date of signing the Contract Agreement.

1.1.1.4   "**Letter of Tender**" means the document entitled letter of tender, which was completed by the Contractor and includes the signed offer to the Employer for the Works.

1.1.1.5   "**Specification**" means the document entitled specification, as included in the Contract, and any additions and modifications to the specification in accordance with the Contract. Such document specifies the Works.

1.1.1.6   "**Drawings**" means the drawings of the Works, as included in the Contract, and any additional and modified drawings issued by (or on behalf of) the Employer in accordance with the Contract.

1.1.1.7   "**Schedules**" means the document(s) entitled schedules, completed by the Contractor and submitted with the Letter of Tender, as included in the Contract. Such document may include the Bill of Quantities, data, lists, and schedules of rates and/or prices.

1.1.1.8   "**Tender**" means the Letter of Tender and all other documents which the Contractor submitted with the Letter of Tender, as included in the Contract.

1.1.1.9   "**Appendix to Tender**" means the completed pages entitled appendix to tender which are appended to and form part of the Letter of Tender.

1.1.1.10 "**Bill of Quantities**" and "**Daywork Schedule**" mean the documents so named (if any) which are comprised in the Schedules.

1.1.2
Parties and Persons

1.1.2.1   "**Party**" means the Employer or the Contractor, as the context requires.

1.1.2.2   "**Employer**" means the person named as employer in the Appendix to Tender and the legal successors in title to this person.

1.1.2.3   "**Contractor**" means the person(s) named as contractor in the Letter of Tender accepted by the Employer and the legal successors in title to this person(s).

1.1.2.4   "**Engineer**" means the person appointed by the Employer to act as the Engineer for the purposes of the Contract and named in the Appendix to Tender, or other person appointed from time to time by the Employer and notified to the Contractor under Sub-Clause 3.4 [*Replacement of the Engineer*].

1.1.2.5   "**Contractor's Representative**" means the person named by the Contractor in the Contract or appointed from time to time by the Contractor under Sub-Clause 4.3 [*Contractor's Representative*], who acts on behalf of the Contractor.

1.1.2.6   "**Employer's Personnel**" means the Engineer, the assistants referred to in Sub-Clause 3.2 [*Delegation by the Engineer*] and all other staff, labour and other employees of the Engineer and of the Employer; and any other personnel notified to the Contractor, by the Employer or the Engineer, as Employer's Personnel.

1.1.2.7   "**Contractor's Personnel**" means the Contractor's Representative and all personnel whom the Contractor utilises on Site, who may include the staff, labour and other employees of the Contractor and of each Subcontractor; and any other personnel assisting the Contractor in the execution of the Works.

1.1.2.8   "**Subcontractor**" means any person named in the Contract as a subcontractor, or any person appointed as a subcontractor, for a part of the Works; and the legal successors in title to each of these persons.

1.1.2.9   "**DAB**" means the person or three persons so named in the Contract, or other person(s) appointed under Sub-Clause 20.2 [*Appointment of the Dispute Adjudication Board*] or Sub-Clause 20.3 [*Failure to Agree Dispute Adjudication Board*]

1.1.2.10   "**FIDIC**" means the Fédération Internationale des Ingénieurs-Conseils, the international federation of consulting engineers.

1.1.3
Dates, Tests, Periods and Completion

1.1.3.1   "**Base Date**" means the date 28 days prior to the latest date for submission of the Tender.

1.1.3.2   "**Commencement Date**" means the date notified under Sub-Clause 8.1 [*Commencement of Works*].

1.1.3.3   "**Time for Completion**" means the time for completing the Works or a Section (as the case may be) under Sub-Clause 8.2 [*Time for Completion*], as stated in the Appendix to Tender (with any extension under Sub-Clause 8.4 [*Extension of Time for Completion*]), calculated from the Commencement Date.

1.1.3.4   "**Tests on Completion**" means the tests which are specified in the Contract or agreed by both Parties or instructed as a Variation, and which are carried

       Conditions of Contract for Construction

out under Clause 9 [*Tests on Completion*] before the Works or a Section (as the case may be) are taken over by the Employer.

1.1.3.5　"**Taking-Over Certificate**" means a certificate issued under Clause 10 [*Employer's Taking Over*].

1.1.3.6　"**Tests after Completion**" means the tests (if any) which are specified in the Contract and which are carried out in accordance with the provisions of the Particular Conditions after the Works or a Section (as the case may be) are taken over by the Employer.

1.1.3.7　"**Defects Notification Period**" means the period for notifying defects in the Works or a Section (as the case may be) under Sub-Clause 11.1 [*Completion of Outstanding Work and Remedying Defects*], as stated in the Appendix to Tender (with any extension under Sub-Clause 11.3 [*Extension of Defects Notification Period*]), calculated from the date on which the Works or Section is completed as certified under Sub-Clause 10.1 [*Taking Over of the Works and Sections*].

1.1.3.8　"**Performance Certificate**" means the certificate issued under Sub-Clause 11.9 [*Performance Certificate*].

1.1.3.9　"**day**" means a calendar day and "**year**" means 365 days.

1.1.4
Money and Payments　1.1.4.1　"**Accepted Contract Amount**" means the amount accepted in the Letter of Acceptance for the execution and completion of the Works and the remedying of any defects.

1.1.4.2　"**Contract Price**" means the price defined in Sub-Clause 14.1 [*The Contract Price*], and includes adjustments in accordance with the Contract.

1.1.4.3　"**Cost**" means all expenditure reasonably incurred (or to be incurred) by the Contractor, whether on or off the Site, including overhead and similar charges, but does not include profit.

1.1.4.4　"**Final Payment Certificate**" means the payment certificate issued under Sub-Clause 14.13 [*Issue of Final Payment Certificate*].

1.1.4.5　"**Final Statement**" means the statement defined in Sub-Clause 14.11 [*Application for Final Payment Certificate*].

1.1.4.6　"**Foreign Currency**" means a currency in which part (or all) of the Contract Price is payable, but not the Local Currency.

1.1.4.7　"**Interim Payment Certificate**" means a payment certificate issued under Clause 14 [*Contract Price and Payment*], other than the Final Payment Certificate.

1.1.4.8　"**Local Currency**" means the currency of the Country.

1.1.4.9　"**Payment Certificate**" means a payment certificate issued under Clause 14 [*Contract Price and Payment*].

1.1.4.10　"**Provisional Sum**" means a sum (if any) which is specified in the Contract as a provisional sum, for the execution of any part of the Works or for the supply of Plant, Materials or services under Sub-Clause 13.5 [*Provisional Sums*].

1.1.4.11   "**Retention Money**" means the accumulated retention moneys which the Employer retains under Sub-Clause 14.3 [*Application for Interim Payment Certificates*] and pays under Sub-Clause 14.9 [*Payment of Retention Money*].

1.1.4.12   "**Statement**" means a statement submitted by the Contractor as part of an application, under Clause 14 [*Contract Price and Payment*], for a payment certificate.

1.1.5
Works and Goods

1.1.5.1   "**Contractor's Equipment**" means all apparatus, machinery, vehicles and other things required for the execution and completion of the Works and the remedying of any defects. However, Contractor's Equipment excludes Temporary Works, Employer's Equipment (if any), Plant, Materials and any other things intended to form or forming part of the Permanent Works.

1.1.5.2   "**Goods**" means Contractor's Equipment, Materials, Plant and Temporary Works, or any of them as appropriate.

1.1.5.3   "**Materials**" means things of all kinds (other than Plant) intended to form or forming part of the Permanent Works, including the supply-only materials (if any) to be supplied by the Contractor under the Contract.

1.1.5.4   "**Permanent Works**" means the permanent works to be executed by the Contractor under the Contract.

1.1.5.5   "**Plant**" means the apparatus, machinery and vehicles intended to form or forming part of the Permanent Works.

1.1.5.6   "**Section**" means a part of the Works specified in the Appendix to Tender as a Section (if any).

1.1.5.7   "**Temporary Works**" means all temporary works of every kind (other than Contractor's Equipment) required on Site for the execution and completion of the Permanent Works and the remedying of any defects.

1.1.5.8   "**Works**" mean the Permanent Works and the Temporary Works, or either of them as appropriate.

1.1.6
Other Definitions

1.1.6.1   "**Contractor's Documents**" means the calculations, computer programs and other software, drawings, manuals, models and other documents of a technical nature (if any) supplied by the Contractor under the Contract.

1.1.6.2   "**Country**" means the country in which the Site (or most of it) is located, where the Permanent Works are to be executed.

1.1.6.3   "**Employer's Equipment**" means the apparatus, machinery and vehicles (if any) made available by the Employer for the use of the Contractor in the execution of the Works, as stated in the Specification; but does not include Plant which has not been taken over by the Employer.

1.1.6.4   "**Force Majeure**" is defined in Clause 19 [*Force Majeure*].

1.1.6.5   "**Laws**" means all national (or state) legislation, statutes, ordinances and other laws, and regulations and by-laws of any legally constituted public authority.

1.1.6.6   "**Performance Security**" means the security (or securities, if any) under Sub-Clause 4.2 [*Performance Security*].

1.1.6.7   "**Site**" means the places where the Permanent Works are to be executed and to which Plant and Materials are to be delivered, and any other places as may be specified in the Contract as forming part of the Site.

1.1.6.8   "**Unforeseeable**" means not reasonably foreseeable by an experienced contractor by the date for submission of the Tender.

1.1.6.9   "**Variation**" means any change to the Works, which is instructed or approved as a variation under Clause 13 [*Variations and Adjustments*].

1.2

Interpretation

In the Contract, except where the context requires otherwise:

(a)   words indicating one gender include all genders;

(b)   words indicating the singular also include the plural and words indicating the plural also include the singular;

(c)   provisions including the word "agree", "agreed" or "agreement" require the agreement to be recorded in writing, and

(d)   "written" or "in writing" means hand-written, type-written, printed or electronically made, and resulting in a permanent record.

The marginal words and other headings shall not be taken into consideration in the interpretation of these Conditions.

1.3

Communications

Wherever these Conditions provide for the giving or issuing of approvals, certificates, consents, determinations, notices and requests, these communications shall be:

(a)   in writing and delivered by hand (against receipt), sent by mail or courier, or transmitted using any of the agreed systems of electronic transmission as stated in the Appendix to Tender; and

(b)   delivered, sent or transmitted to the address for the recipient's communications as stated in the Appendix to Tender. However:

    (i)   if the recipient gives notice of another address, communications shall thereafter be delivered accordingly; and

    (ii)   if the recipient has not stated otherwise when requesting an approval or consent, it may be sent to the address from which the request was issued.

Approvals, certificates, consents and determinations shall not be unreasonably withheld or delayed. When a certificate is issued to a Party, the certifier shall send a copy to the other Party. When a notice is issued to a Party, by the other Party or the Engineer, a copy shall be sent to the Engineer or the other Party, as the case may be.

1.4

Law and Language

The Contract shall be governed by the law of the country (or other jurisdiction) stated in the Appendix to Tender.

If there are versions of any part of the Contract which are written in more than one language, the version which is in the ruling language stated in the Appendix to Tender shall prevail.

The language for communications shall be that stated in the Appendix to Tender. If no language is stated there, the language for communications shall be the language in which the Contract (or most of it) is written.

1.5

Priority of Documents

The documents forming the Contract are to be taken as mutually explanatory of one another. For the purposes of interpretation, the priority of the documents shall be in accordance with the following sequence:

(a)   the Contract Agreement (if any),
(b)   the Letter of Acceptance,
(c)   the Letter of Tender,
(d)   the Particular Conditions,
(e)   these General Conditions,
(f)   the Specification,
(g)   the Drawings, and
(h)   the Schedules and any other documents forming part of the Contract.

If an ambiguity or discrepancy is found in the documents, the Engineer shall issue any necessary clarification or instruction.

1.6

Contract Agreement

The Parties shall enter into a Contract Agreement within 28 days after the Contractor receives the Letter of Acceptance, unless they agree otherwise. The Contract Agreement shall be based upon the form annexed to the Particular Conditions. The costs of stamp duties and similar charges (if any) imposed by law in connection with entry into the Contract Agreement shall be borne by the Employer.

1.7

Assignment

Neither Party shall assign the whole or any part of the Contract or any benefit or interest in or under the Contract. However, either Party:

(a)   may assign the whole or any part with the prior agreement of the other Party, at the sole discretion of such other Party, and
(b)   may, as security in favour of a bank or financial institution, assign its right to any moneys due, or to become due, under the Contract.

1.8

Care and Supply of Documents

The Specification and Drawings shall be in the custody and care of the Employer. Unless otherwise stated in the Contract, two copies of the Contract and of each subsequent Drawing shall be supplied to the Contractor, who may make or request further copies at the cost of the Contractor.

Each of the Contractor's Documents shall be in the custody and care of the Contractor, unless and until taken over by the Employer. Unless otherwise stated in the Contract, the Contractor shall supply to the Engineer six copies of each of the Contractor's Documents.

The Contractor shall keep, on the Site, a copy of the Contract, publications named in the Specification, the Contractor's Documents (if any), the Drawings and Variations and other communications given under the Contract. The Employer's Personnel shall have the right of access to all these documents at all reasonable times.

If a Party becomes aware of an error or defect of a technical nature in a document which was prepared for use in executing the Works, the Party shall promptly give notice to the other Party of such error or defect.

1.9
Delayed Drawings or
Instructions

The Contractor shall give notice to the Engineer whenever the Works are likely to be delayed or disrupted if any necessary drawing or instruction is not issued to the Contractor within a particular time, which shall be reasonable. The notice shall include details of the necessary drawing or instruction, details of why and by when it should be issued, and details of the nature and amount of the delay or disruption likely to be suffered if it is late.

If the Contractor suffers delay and/or incurs Cost as a result of a failure of the Engineer to issue the notified drawing or instruction within a time which is reasonable and is specified in the notice with supporting details, the Contractor shall give a further notice to the Engineer and shall be entitled subject to Sub-Clause 20.1 [*Contractor's Claims*] to:

(a)   an extension of time for any such delay, if completion is or will be delayed, under Sub-Clause 8.4 [*Extension of Time for Completion*], and

(b)   payment of any such Cost plus reasonable profit, which shall be included in the Contract Price.

After receiving this further notice, the Engineer shall proceed in accordance with Sub-Clause 3.5 [*Determinations*] to agree or determine these matters.

However, if and to the extent that the Engineer's failure was caused by any error or delay by the Contractor, including an error in, or delay in the submission of, any of the Contractor's Documents, the Contractor shall not be entitled to such extension of time, Cost or profit.

1.10

Employer's Use of
Contractor's Documents

As between the Parties, the Contractor shall retain the copyright and other intellectual property rights in the Contractor's Documents and other design documents made by (or on behalf of) the Contractor.

The Contractor shall be deemed (by signing the Contract) to give to the Employer a non-terminable transferable non-exclusive royalty-free licence to copy, use and communicate the Contractor's Documents, including making and using modifications of them. This licence shall:

(a)   apply throughout the actual or intended working life (whichever is longer) of the relevant parts of the Works,

(b)   entitle any person in proper possession of the relevant part of the Works to copy, use and communicate the Contractor's Documents for the purposes of completing, operating, maintaining, altering, adjusting, repairing and demolishing the Works, and

(c)   in the case of Contractor's Documents which are in the form of computer programs and other software, permit their use on any computer on the Site and other places as envisaged by the Contract, including replacements of any computers supplied by the Contractor.

The Contractor's Documents and other design documents made by (or on behalf of) the Contractor shall not, without the Contractor's consent, be used, copied or communicated to a third party by (or on behalf of) the Employer for purposes other than those permitted under this Sub-Clause.

1.11

Contractor's Use of
Employer's Documents

As between the Parties, the Employer shall retain the copyright and other intellectual property rights in the Specification, the Drawings and other documents made by (or on behalf of) the Employer. The Contractor may, at his cost, copy, use, and obtain communication of these documents for the purposes of the Contract. They shall not, without the Employer's consent, be copied, used or communicated to a third party by the Contractor, except as necessary for the purposes of the Contract.

1.12

Confidential Details

The Contractor shall disclose all such confidential and other information as the Engineer may reasonably require in order to verify the Contractor's compliance with the Contract.

1.13

Compliance with Laws

The Contractor shall, in performing the Contract, comply with applicable Laws. Unless otherwise stated in the Particular Conditions:

(a)   the Employer shall have obtained (or shall obtain) the planning, zoning or similar permission for the Permanent Works, and any other permissions described in the Specification as having been (or being) obtained by the Employer; and the Employer shall indemnify and hold the Contractor harmless against and from the consequences of any failure to do so; and

(b)   the Contractor shall give all notices, pay all taxes, duties and fees, and obtain all permits, licences and approvals, as required by the Laws in relation to the execution and completion of the Works and the remedying of any defects; and the Contractor shall indemnify and hold the Employer harmless against and from the consequences of any failure to do so.

1.14

Joint and Several Liability

If the Contractor constitutes (under applicable Laws) a joint venture, consortium or other unincorporated grouping of two or more persons:

(a)   these persons shall be deemed to be jointly and severally liable to the Employer for the performance of the Contract;

(b)   these persons shall notify the Employer of their leader who shall have authority to bind the Contractor and each of these persons; and

(c)   the Contractor shall not alter its composition or legal status without the prior consent of the Employer.

The 2 Employer

2.1

Right of Access to the Site

The Employer shall give the Contractor right of access to, and possession of, all parts of the Site within the time (or times) stated in the Appendix to Tender. The right and possession may not be exclusive to the Contractor. If, under the Contract, the Employer is required to give (to the Contractor) possession of any foundation, structure, plant or means of access, the Employer shall do so in the time and manner stated in the Specification. However, the Employer may withhold any such right or possession until the Performance Security has been received.

If no such time is stated in the Appendix to Tender, the Employer shall give the Contractor right of access to, and possession of, the Site within such times as may be required to enable the Contractor to proceed in accordance with the programme submitted under Sub-Clause 8.3 [*Programme*].

If the Contractor suffers delay and/or incurs Cost as a result of a failure by the Employer to give any such right or possession within such time, the Contractor shall give notice to the Engineer and shall be entitled subject to Sub-Clause 20.1 [*Contractor's Claims*] to:

Conditions of Contract for Construction

(a)   an extension of time for any such delay, if completion is or will be delayed, under Sub-Clause 8.4 [*Extension of Time for Completion*], and

(b)   payment of any such Cost plus reasonable profit, which shall be included in the Contract Price.

After receiving this notice, the Engineer shall proceed in accordance with Sub-Clause 3.5 [*Determinations*] to agree or determine these matters.

However, if and to the extent that the Employer's failure was caused by any error or delay by the Contractor, including an error in, or delay in the submission of, any of the Contractor's Documents, the Contractor shall not be entitled to such extension of time, Cost or profit.

2.2

Permits, Licences or Approvals

The Employer shall (where he is in a position to do so) provide reasonable assistance to the Contractor at the request of the Contractor:

(a)   by obtaining copies of the Laws of the Country which are relevant to the Contract but are not readily available, and

(b)   for the Contractor's applications for any permits, licences or approvals required by the Laws of the Country:

(i)   which the Contractor is required to obtain under Sub-Clause 1.13 [*Compliance with Laws*],

(ii)   for the delivery of Goods, including clearance through customs, and

(iii)   for the export of Contractor's Equipment when it is removed from the Site.

2.3

Employer's Personnel

The Employer shall be responsible for ensuring that the Employer's Personnel and the Employer's other contractors on the Site:

(a)   co-operate with the Contractor's efforts under Sub-Clause 4.6 [*Co-operation*], and

(b)   take actions similar to those which the Contractor is required to take under sub-paragraphs (a), (b) and (c) of Sub-Clause 4.8 [*Safety Procedures*] and under Sub-Clause 4.18 [*Protection of the Environment*].

2.4

Employer's Financial Arrangements

The Employer shall submit, within 28 days after receiving any request from the Contractor, reasonable evidence that financial arrangements have been made and are being maintained which will enable the Employer to pay the Contract Price (as estimated at that time) in accordance with Clause 14 [*Contract Price and Payment*]. If the Employer intends to make any material change to his financial arrangements, the Employer shall give notice to the Contractor with detailed particulars.

2.5

Employer's Claims

If the Employer considers himself to be entitled to any payment under any Clause of these Conditions or otherwise in connection with the Contract, and/or to any extension of the Defects Notification Period, the Employer or the Engineer shall give notice and particulars to the Contractor. However, notice is not required for payments due under Sub-Clause 4.19 [*Electricity, Water and Gas*], under Sub-Clause 4.20 [*Employer's Equipment and Free-Issue Material*], or for other services requested by the Contractor.

The notice shall be given as soon as practicable after the Employer became aware of the event or circumstances giving rise to the claim. A notice relating to any extension of the Defects Notification Period shall be given before the expiry of such period.

The particulars shall specify the Clause or other basis of the claim, and shall include substantiation of the amount and/or extension to which the Employer considers himself to be entitled in connection with the Contract. The Engineer shall then proceed in accordance with Sub-Clause 3.5 [*Determinations*] to agree or determine (i) the amount (if any) which the Employer is entitled to be paid by the Contractor, and/or (ii) the extension (if any) of the Defects Notification Period in accordance with Sub-Clause 11.3 [*Extension of Defects Notification Period*].

This amount may be included as a deduction in the Contract Price and Payment Certificates. The Employer shall only be entitled to set off against or make any deduction from an amount certified in a Payment Certificate, or to otherwise claim against the Contractor, in accordance with this Sub-Clause.

The 3 Engineer

3.1
Engineer's Duties and Authority

The Employer shall appoint the Engineer who shall carry out the duties assigned to him in the Contract. The Engineer's staff shall include suitably qualified engineers and other professionals who are competent to carry out these duties.

The Engineer shall have no authority to amend the Contract.

The Engineer may exercise the authority attributable to the Engineer as specified in or necessarily to be implied from the Contract. If the Engineer is required to obtain the approval of the Employer before exercising a specified authority, the requirements shall be as stated in the Particular Conditions. The Employer undertakes not to impose further constraints on the Engineer's authority, except as agreed with the Contractor.

However, whenever the Engineer exercises a specified authority for which the Employer's approval is required, then (for the purposes of the Contract) the Employer shall be deemed to have given approval.

Except as otherwise stated in these Conditions:

(a)   whenever carrying out duties or exercising authority, specified in or implied by the Contract, the Engineer shall be deemed to act for the Employer;

(b)   the Engineer has no authority to relieve either Party of any duties, obligations or responsibilities under the Contract; and

(c)   any approval, check, certificate, consent, examination, inspection, instruction, notice, proposal, request, test, or similar act by the Engineer (including absence of disapproval) shall not relieve the Contractor from any responsibility he has under the Contract, including responsibility for errors, omissions, discrepancies and non-compliances.

3.2
Delegation by the Engineer

The Engineer may from time to time assign duties and delegate authority to assistants, and may also revoke such assignment or delegation. These assistants may include a resident engineer, and/or independent inspectors appointed to inspect and/or test items of Plant and/or Materials. The assignment, delegation or revocation shall be in writing and shall not take effect until copies have been received by both Parties. However, unless otherwise agreed by both Parties, the Engineer shall not delegate the authority to determine any matter in accordance with Sub-Clause 3.5 [*Determinations*].

Assistants shall be suitably qualified persons, who are competent to carry out these duties and exercise this authority, and who are fluent in the language for communications defined in Sub-Clause 1.4 [*Law and Language*].

Each assistant, to whom duties have been assigned or authority has been delegated, shall only be authorised to issue instructions to the Contractor to the extent defined by the delegation. Any approval, check, certificate, consent, examination, inspection, instruction, notice, proposal, request, test, or similar act by an assistant, in accordance with the delegation, shall have the same effect as though the act had been an act of the Engineer. However:

(a) any failure to disapprove any work, Plant or Materials shall not constitute approval, and shall therefore not prejudice the right of the Engineer to reject the work, Plant or Materials;

(b) if the Contractor questions any determination or instruction of an assistant, the Contractor may refer the matter to the Engineer, who shall promptly confirm, reverse or vary the determination or instruction.

3.3

Instructions of the Engineer

The Engineer may issue to the Contractor (at any time) instructions and additional or modified Drawings which may be necessary for the execution of the Works and the remedying of any defects, all in accordance with the Contract. The Contractor shall only take instructions from the Engineer, or from an assistant to whom the appropriate authority has been delegated under this Clause. If an instruction constitutes a Variation, Clause 13 [*Variations and Adjustments*] shall apply.

The Contractor shall comply with the instructions given by the Engineer or delegated assistant, on any matter related to the Contract. Whenever practicable, their instructions shall be given in writing. If the Engineer or a delegated assistant:

(a) gives an oral instruction,

(b) receives a written confirmation of the instruction, from (or on behalf of) the Contractor, within two working days after giving the instruction, and

(c) does not reply by issuing a written rejection and/or instruction within two working days after receiving the confirmation,

then the confirmation shall constitute the written instruction of the Engineer or delegated assistant (as the case may be).

3.4

Replacement of the Engineer

If the Employer intends to replace the Engineer, the Employer shall, not less than 42 days before the intended date of replacement, give notice to the Contractor of the name, address and relevant experience of the intended replacement Engineer. The Employer shall not replace the Engineer with a person against whom the Contractor raises reasonable objection by notice to the Employer, with supporting particulars.

3.5

Determinations

Whenever these Conditions provide that the Engineer shall proceed in accordance with this Sub-Clause 3.5 to agree or determine any matter, the Engineer shall consult with each Party in an endeavour to reach agreement. If agreement is not achieved, the Engineer shall make a fair determination in accordance with the Contract, taking due regard of all relevant circumstances.

The Engineer shall give notice to both Parties of each agreement or determination, with supporting particulars. Each Party shall give effect to each agreement or determination unless and until revised under Clause 20 [*Claims, Disputes and Arbitration*].

The 4 Contractor

4.1

Contractor's General Obligations

The Contractor shall design (to the extent specified in the Contract), execute and complete the Works in accordance with the Contract and with the Engineer's instructions, and shall remedy any defects in the Works.

The Contractor shall provide the Plant and Contractor's Documents specified in the Contract, and all Contractor's Personnel, Goods, consumables and other things and services, whether of a temporary or permanent nature, required in and for this design, execution, completion and remedying of defects.

The Contractor shall be responsible for the adequacy, stability and safety of all Site operations and of all methods of construction. Except to the extent specified in the Contract, the Contractor (i) shall be responsible for all Contractor's Documents, Temporary Works, and such design of each item of Plant and Materials as is required for the item to be in accordance with the Contract, and (ii) shall not otherwise be responsible for the design or specification of the Permanent Works.

The Contractor shall, whenever required by the Engineer, submit details of the arrangements and methods which the Contractor proposes to adopt for the execution of the Works. No significant alteration to these arrangements and methods shall be made without this having previously been notified to the Engineer.

If the Contract specifies that the Contractor shall design any part of the Permanent Works, then unless otherwise stated in the Particular Conditions:

(a) the Contractor shall submit to the Engineer the Contractor's Documents for this part in accordance with the procedures specified in the Contract;

(b) these Contractor's Documents shall be in accordance with the Specification and Drawings, shall be written in the language for communications defined in Sub-Clause 1.4 [*Law and Language*], and shall include additional information required by the Engineer to add to the Drawings for co-ordination of each Party's designs;

(c) the Contractor shall be responsible for this part and it shall, when the Works are completed, be fit for such purposes for which the part is intended as are specified in the Contract; and

(d) prior to the commencement of the Tests on Completion, the Contractor shall submit to the Engineer the "as-built" documents and operation and maintenance manuals in accordance with the Specification and in sufficient detail for the Employer to operate, maintain, dismantle, reassemble, adjust and repair this part of the Works. Such part shall not be considered to be completed for the purposes of taking-over under Sub-Clause 10.1 [*Taking Over of the Works and Sections*] until these documents and manuals have been submitted to the Engineer.

4.2

Performance Security

The Contractor shall obtain (at his cost) a Performance Security for proper performance, in the amount and currencies stated in the Appendix to Tender. If an amount is not stated in the Appendix to Tender, this Sub-Clause shall not apply.

The Contractor shall deliver the Performance Security to the Employer within 28 days after receiving the Letter of Acceptance, and shall send a copy to the Engineer. The Performance Security shall be issued by an entity and from within a country (or other jurisdiction) approved by the Employer, and shall be in the form annexed to the Particular Conditions or in another form approved by the Employer.

The Contractor shall ensure that the Performance Security is valid and enforceable until the Contractor has executed and completed the Works and remedied any defects. If the terms of the Performance Security specify its expiry date, and the Contractor has not become entitled to receive the Performance Certificate by the date 28 days prior to the expiry date, the Contractor shall extend the validity of the Performance Security until the Works have been completed and any defects have been remedied.

The Employer shall not make a claim under the Performance Security, except for amounts to which the Employer is entitled under the Contract in the event of:

(a)   failure by the Contractor to extend the validity of the Performance Security as described in the preceding paragraph, in which event the Employer may claim the full amount of the Performance Security,

(b)   failure by the Contractor to pay the Employer an amount due, as either agreed by the Contractor or determined under Sub-Clause 2.5 [*Employer's Claims*] or Clause 20 [*Claims, Disputes and Arbitration*], within 42 days after this agreement or determination,

(c)   failure by the Contractor to remedy a default within 42 days after receiving the Employer's notice requiring the default to be remedied, or

(d)   circumstances which entitle the Employer to termination under Sub-Clause 15.2 [*Termination by Employer*], irrespective of whether notice of termination has been given.

The Employer shall indemnify and hold the Contractor harmless against and from all damages, losses and expenses (including legal fees and expenses) resulting from a claim under the Performance Security to the extent to which the Employer was not entitled to make the claim.

The Employer shall return the Performance Security to the Contractor within 21 days after receiving a copy of the Performance Certificate.

4.3

Contractor's Representative

The Contractor shall appoint the Contractor's Representative and shall give him all authority necessary to act on the Contractor's behalf under the Contract.

Unless the Contractor's Representative is named in the Contract, the Contractor shall, prior to the Commencement Date, submit to the Engineer for consent the name and particulars of the person the Contractor proposes to appoint as Contractor's Representative. If consent is withheld or subsequently revoked, or if the appointed person fails to act as Contractor's Representative, the Contractor shall similarly submit the name and particulars of another suitable person for such appointment.

The Contractor shall not, without the prior consent of the Engineer, revoke the appointment of the Contractor's Representative or appoint a replacement.

The whole time of the Contractor's Representative shall be given to directing the Contractor's performance of the Contract. If the Contractor's Representative is to be temporarily absent from the Site during the execution of the Works, a suitable replacement person shall be appointed, subject to the Engineer's prior consent, and the Engineer shall be notified accordingly.

The Contractor's Representative shall, on behalf of the Contractor, receive instructions under Sub-Clause 3.3 [*Instructions of the Engineer*].

The Contractor's Representative may delegate any powers, functions and authority to any competent person, and may at any time revoke the delegation. Any delegation or revocation shall not take effect until the Engineer has received prior notice signed by the Contractor's Representative, naming the person and specifying the powers, functions and authority being delegated or revoked.

The Contractor's Representative and all these persons shall be fluent in the language for communications defined in Sub-Clause 1.4 [*Law and Language*].

4.4

Subcontractors

The Contractor shall not subcontract the whole of the Works.

The Contractor shall be responsible for the acts or defaults of any Subcontractor, his agents or employees, as if they were the acts or defaults of the Contractor. Unless otherwise stated in the Particular Conditions:

(a) the Contractor shall not be required to obtain consent to suppliers of Materials, or to a subcontract for which the Subcontractor is named in the Contract;

(b) the prior consent of the Engineer shall be obtained to other proposed Subcontractors;

(c) the Contractor shall give the Engineer not less than 28 days' notice of the intended date of the commencement of each Subcontractor's work, and of the commencement of such work on the Site; and

(d) each subcontract shall include provisions which would entitle the Employer to require the subcontract to be assigned to the Employer under Sub-Clause 4.5 [*Assignment of Benefit of Subcontract*] (if or when applicable) or in the event of termination under Sub-Clause 15.2 [*Termination by Employer*].

4.5

Assignment of Benefit of Subcontract

If a Subcontractor's obligations extend beyond the expiry date of the relevant Defects Notification Period and the Engineer, prior to this date, instructs the Contractor to assign the benefit of such obligations to the Employer, then the Contractor shall do so. Unless otherwise stated in the assignment, the Contractor shall have no liability to the Employer for the work carried out by the Subcontractor after the assignment takes effect.

4.6

Co-operation

The Contractor shall, as specified in the Contract or as instructed by the Engineer, allow appropriate opportunities for carrying out work to:

(a) the Employer's Personnel,

(b) any other contractors employed by the Employer, and

(c) the personnel of any legally constituted public authorities,

who may be employed in the execution on or near the Site of any work not included in the Contract.

Any such instruction shall constitute a Variation if and to the extent that it causes the Contractor to incur Unforeseeable Cost. Services for these personnel and other contractors may include the use of Contractor's Equipment, Temporary Works or access arrangements which are the responsibility of the Contractor.

If, under the Contract, the Employer is required to give to the Contractor possession of any foundation, structure, plant or means of access in accordance with Contractor's Documents, the Contractor shall submit such documents to the Engineer in the time and manner stated in the Specification.

4.7
Setting Out

The Contractor shall set out the Works in relation to original points, lines and levels of reference specified in the Contract or notified by the Engineer. The Contractor shall be responsible for the correct positioning of all parts of the Works, and shall rectify any error in the positions, levels, dimensions or alignment of the Works.

The Employer shall be responsible for any errors in these specified or notified items of reference, but the Contractor shall use reasonable efforts to verify their accuracy before they are used.

If the Contractor suffers delay and/or incurs Cost from executing work which was necessitated by an error in these items of reference, and an experienced contractor could not reasonably have discovered such error and avoided this delay and/or Cost, the Contractor shall give notice to the Engineer and shall be entitled subject to Sub-Clause 20.1 [*Contractor's Claims*] to:

(a) an extension of time for any such delay, if completion is or will be delayed, under Sub-Clause 8.4 [*Extension of Time for Completion*], and

(b) payment of any such Cost plus reasonable profit, which shall be included in the Contract Price.

After receiving this notice, the Engineer shall proceed in accordance with Sub-Clause 3.5 [*Determinations*] to agree or determine (i) whether and (if so) to what extent the error could not reasonably have been discovered, and (ii) the matters described in sub-paragraphs (a) and (b) above related to this extent.

4.8
Safety Procedures

The Contractor shall:

(a) comply with all applicable safety regulations,

(b) take care for the safety of all persons entitled to be on the Site,

(c) use reasonable efforts to keep the Site and Works clear of unnecessary obstruction so as to avoid danger to these persons,

(d) provide fencing, lighting, guarding and watching of the Works until completion and taking over under Clause 10 [*Employer's Taking Over*], and

(e) provide any Temporary Works (including roadways, footways, guards and fences) which may be necessary, because of the execution of the Works, for the use and protection of the public and of owners and occupiers of adjacent land.

4.9
Quality Assurance

The Contractor shall institute a quality assurance system to demonstrate compliance with the requirements of the Contract. The system shall be in accordance with the details stated in the Contract. The Engineer shall be entitled to audit any aspect of the system.

Details of all procedures and compliance documents shall be submitted to the Engineer for information before each design and execution stage is commenced. When any document of a technical nature is issued to the Engineer, evidence of the prior approval by the Contractor himself shall be apparent on the document itself.

Compliance with the quality assurance system shall not relieve the Contractor of any of his duties, obligations or responsibilities under the Contract.

4.10
Site Data

The Employer shall have made available to the Contractor for his information, prior to the Base Date, all relevant data in the Employer's possession on sub-surface and hydrological conditions at the Site, including environmental aspects. The Employer shall similarly make available to the Contractor all such data which come into the Employer's possession after the Base Date. The Contractor shall be responsible for interpreting all such data.

To the extent which was practicable (taking account of cost and time), the Contractor shall be deemed to have obtained all necessary information as to risks, contingencies and other circumstances which may influence or affect the Tender or Works. To the same extent, the Contractor shall be deemed to have inspected and examined the Site, its surroundings, the above data and other available information, and to have been satisfied before submitting the Tender as to all relevant matters, including (without limitation):

(a)   the form and nature of the Site, including sub-surface conditions,
(b)   the hydrological and climatic conditions,
(c)   the extent and nature of the work and Goods necessary for the execution and completion of the Works and the remedying of any defects,
(d)   the Laws, procedures and labour practices of the Country, and
(e)   the Contractor's requirements for access, accommodation, facilities, personnel, power, transport, water and other services.

4.11

Sufficiency of the Accepted Contract Amount

The Contractor shall be deemed to:

(a)   have satisfied himself as to the correctness and sufficiency of the Accepted Contract Amount, and
(b)   have based the Accepted Contract Amount on the data, interpretations, necessary information, inspections, examinations and satisfaction as to all relevant matters referred to in Sub-Clause 4.10 [*Site Data*].

Unless otherwise stated in the Contract, the Accepted Contract Amount covers all the Contractor's obligations under the Contract (including those under Provisional Sums, if any) and all things necessary for the proper execution and completion of the Works and the remedying of any defects.

4.12

Unforeseeable Physical Conditions

In this Sub-Clause, "physical conditions" means natural physical conditions and man-made and other physical obstructions and pollutants, which the Contractor encounters at the Site when executing the Works, including sub-surface and hydro-logical conditions but excluding climatic conditions.

If the Contractor encounters adverse physical conditions which he considers to have been Unforeseeable, the Contractor shall give notice to the Engineer as soon as practicable.

This notice shall describe the physical conditions, so that they can be inspected by the Engineer, and shall set out the reasons why the Contractor considers them to be Unforeseeable. The Contractor shall continue executing the Works, using such proper and reasonable measures as are appropriate for the physical conditions, and shall comply with any instructions which the Engineer may give. If an instruction constitutes a Variation, Clause 13 [*Variations and Adjustments*] shall apply.

If and to the extent that the Contractor encounters physical conditions which are Unfore-seeable, gives such a notice, and suffers delay and/or incurs Cost due to these conditions, the Contractor shall be entitled subject to Sub-Clause 20.1 [*Contractor's Claims*] to:

(a)   an extension of time for any such delay, if completion is or will be delayed, under Sub-Clause 8.4 [*Extension of Time for Completion*], and
(b)   payment of any such Cost, which shall be included in the Contract Price.

Conditions of Contract for Construction

After receiving such notice and inspecting and/or investigating these physical conditions, the Engineer shall proceed in accordance with Sub-Clause 3.5 [*Determinations*] to agree or determine (i) whether and (if so) to what extent these physical conditions were Unforeseeable, and (ii) the matters described in sub-paragraphs (a) and (b) above related to this extent.

However, before additional Cost is finally agreed or determined under sub-paragraph (ii), the Engineer may also review whether other physical conditions in similar parts of the Works (if any) were more favourable than could reasonably have been foreseen when the Contractor submitted the Tender. If and to the extent that these more favourable conditions were encountered, the Engineer may proceed in accordance with Sub-Clause 3.5 [*Determinations*] to agree or determine the reductions in Cost which were due to these conditions, which may be included (as deductions) in the Contract Price and Payment Certificates. However, the net effect of all adjustments under sub-paragraph (b) and all these reductions, for all the physical conditions encountered in similar parts of the Works, shall not result in a net reduction in the Contract Price.

The Engineer may take account of any evidence of the physical conditions foreseen by the Contractor when submitting the Tender, which may be made available by the Contractor, but shall not be bound by any such evidence.

4.13

Rights of Way and Facilities

The Contractor shall bear all costs and charges for special and/or temporary rights-of-way which he may require, including those for access to the Site. The Contractor shall also obtain, at his risk and cost, any additional facilities outside the Site which he may require for the purposes of the Works.

4.14

Avoidance of Interference

The Contractor shall not interfere unnecessarily or improperly with:

(a)   the convenience of the public, or
(b)   the access to and use and occupation of all roads and footpaths, irrespective of whether they are public or in the possession of the Employer or of others.

The Contractor shall indemnify and hold the Employer harmless against and from all damages, losses and expenses (including legal fees and expenses) resulting from any such unnecessary or improper interference.

4.15

Access Route

The Contractor shall be deemed to have been satisfied as to the suitability and availability of access routes to the Site. The Contractor shall use reasonable efforts to prevent any road or bridge from being damaged by the Contractor's traffic or by the Contractor's Personnel. These efforts shall include the proper use of appropriate vehicles and routes.

Except as otherwise stated in these Conditions:

(a)   the Contractor shall (as between the Parties) be responsible for any maintenance which may be required for his use of access routes;
(b)   the Contractor shall provide all necessary signs or directions along access routes, and shall obtain any permission which may be required from the relevant authorities for his use of routes, signs and directions;
(c)   the Employer shall not be responsible for any claims which may arise from the use or otherwise of any access route,

(d)   the Employer does not guarantee the suitability or availability of particular access routes, and

(e)   Costs due to non-suitability or non-availability, for the use required by the Contractor, of access routes shall be borne by the Contractor.

4.16

Transport of Goods

Unless otherwise stated in the Particular Conditions:

(a)   the Contractor shall give the Engineer not less than 21 days' notice of the date on which any Plant or a major item of other Goods will be delivered to the Site;

(b)   the Contractor shall be responsible for packing, loading, transporting, receiving, unloading, storing and protecting all Goods and other things required for the Works; and

(c)   the Contractor shall indemnify and hold the Employer harmless against and from all damages, losses and expenses (including legal fees and expenses) resulting from the transport of Goods, and shall negotiate and pay all claims arising from their transport.

4.17

Contractor's Equipment

The Contractor shall be responsible for all Contractor's Equipment. When brought on to the Site, Contractor's Equipment shall be deemed to be exclusively intended for the execution of the Works. The Contractor shall not remove from the Site any major items of Contractor's Equipment without the consent of the Engineer. However, consent shall not be required for vehicles transporting Goods or Contractor's Personnel off Site.

4.18

Protection of the Environment

The Contractor shall take all reasonable steps to protect the environment (both on and off the Site) and to limit damage and nuisance to people and property resulting from pollution, noise and other results of his operations.

The Contractor shall ensure that emissions, surface discharges and effluent from the Contractor's activities shall not exceed the values indicated in the Specification, and shall not exceed the values prescribed by applicable Laws.

4.19

Electricity, Water and Gas

The Contractor shall, except as stated below, be responsible for the provision of all power, water and other services he may require.

The Contractor shall be entitled to use for the purposes of the Works such supplies of electricity, water, gas and other services as may be available on the Site and of which details and prices are given in the Specification. The Contractor shall, at his risk and cost, provide any apparatus necessary for his use of these services and for measuring the quantities consumed.

The quantities consumed and the amounts due (at these prices) for such services shall be agreed or determined by the Engineer in accordance with Sub-Clause 2.5 [Employer's Claims] and Sub-Clause 3.5 [Determinations]. The Contractor shall pay these amounts to the Employer.

4.20

Employer's Equipment and Free-Issue Material

The Employer shall make the Employer's Equipment (if any) available for the use of the Contractor in the execution of the Works in accordance with the details, arrangements and prices stated in the Specification. Unless otherwise stated in the Specification:

(a)   the Employer shall be responsible for the Employer's Equipment, except that

(b)   the Contractor shall be responsible for each item of Employer's Equipment whilst any of the Contractor's Personnel is operating it, driving it, directing it or in possession or control of it.

The appropriate quantities and the amounts due (at such stated prices) for the use of Employer's Equipment shall be agreed or determined by the Engineer in accordance with Sub-Clause 2.5 [*Employer's Claims*] and Sub-Clause 3.5 [*Determinations*]. The Contractor shall pay these amounts to the Employer.

The Employer shall supply, free of charge, the "free-issue materials" (if any) in accordance with the details stated in the Specification. The Employer shall, at his risk and cost, provide these materials at the time and place specified in the Contract. The Contractor shall then visually inspect them, and shall promptly give notice to the Engineer of any shortage, defect or default in these materials. Unless otherwise agreed by both Parties, the Employer shall immediately rectify the notified shortage, defect or default.

After this visual inspection, the free-issue materials shall come under the care, custody and control of the Contractor. The Contractor's obligations of inspection, care, custody and control shall not relieve the Employer of liability for any shortage, defect or default not apparent from a visual inspection.

4.21

Progress Reports

Unless otherwise stated in the Particular Conditions, monthly progress reports shall be prepared by the Contractor and submitted to the Engineer in six copies. The first report shall cover the period up to the end of the first calendar month following the Commencement Date. Reports shall be submitted monthly thereafter, each within 7 days after the last day of the period to which it relates.

Reporting shall continue until the Contractor has completed all work which is known to be outstanding at the completion date stated in the Taking-Over Certificate for the Works.

Each report shall include:

(a)   charts and detailed descriptions of progress, including each stage of design (if any), Contractor's Documents, procurement, manufacture, delivery to Site, construction, erection and testing; and including these stages for work by each nominated Subcontractor (as defined in Clause 5 [*Nominated Subcontractors*]),

(b)   photographs showing the status of manufacture and of progress on the Site;

(c)   for the manufacture of each main item of Plant and Materials, the name of the manufacturer, manufacture location, percentage progress, and the actual or expected dates of:

     (i)   commencement of manufacture,
     (ii)   Contractor's inspections,
     (iii)   tests, and
     (iv)   shipment and arrival at the Site;

(d)   the details described in Sub-Clause 6.10 [*Records of Contractor's Personnel and Equipment*];

(e)   copies of quality assurance documents, test results and certificates of Materials;

(f)   list of notices given under Sub-Clause 2.5 [*Employer's Claims*] and notices given under Sub-Clause 20.1 [*Contractor's Claims*];

(g)   safety statistics, including details of any hazardous incidents and activities relating to environmental aspects and public relations; and

(h)   comparisons of actual and planned progress, with details of any events or circumstances which may jeopardise the completion in accordance with the Contract, and the measures being (or to be) adopted to overcome delays.

4.22

Security of the Site

Unless otherwise stated in the Particular Conditions:

(a)   the Contractor shall be responsible for keeping unauthorised persons off the Site, and

(b)   authorised persons shall be limited to the Contractor's Personnel and the Employer's Personnel; and to any other personnel notified to the Contractor, by the Employer or the Engineer, as authorised personnel of the Employer's other contractors on the Site.

4.23

Contractor's Operations on Site

The Contractor shall confine his operations to the Site, and to any additional areas which may be obtained by the Contractor and agreed by the Engineer as working areas. The Contractor shall take all necessary precautions to keep Contractor's Equipment and Contractor's Personnel within the Site and these additional areas, and to keep them off adjacent land.

During the execution of the Works, the Contractor shall keep the Site free from all unnecessary obstruction, and shall store or dispose of any Contractor's Equipment or surplus materials. The Contractor shall clear away and remove from the Site any wreckage, rubbish and Temporary Works which are no longer required.

Upon the issue of a Taking-Over Certificate, the Contractor shall clear away and remove, from that part of the Site and Works to which the Taking-Over Certificate refers, all Contractor's Equipment, surplus material, wreckage, rubbish and Temporary Works. The Contractor shall leave that part of the Site and the Works in a clean and safe condition. However, the Contractor may retain on Site, during the Defects Notification Period, such Goods as are required for the Contractor to fulfil obligations under the Contract.

4.24

Fossils

All fossils, coins, articles of value or antiquity, and structures and other remains or items of geological or archaeological interest found on the Site shall be placed under the care and authority of the Employer. The Contractor shall take reasonable precautions to prevent Contractor's Personnel or other persons from removing or damaging any of these findings.

The Contractor shall, upon discovery of any such finding, promptly give notice to the Engineer, who shall issue instructions for dealing with it. If the Contractor suffers delay and/or incurs Cost from complying with the instructions, the Contractor shall give a further notice to the Engineer and shall be entitled subject to Sub-Clause 20.1 [*Contractor's Claims*] to:

(a)   an extension of time for any such delay, if completion is or will be delayed, under Sub-Clause 8.4 [*Extension of Time for Completion*], and

(b)   payment of any such Cost, which shall be included in the Contract Price.

After receiving this further notice, the Engineer shall proceed in accordance with Sub-Clause 3.5 [*Determinations*] to agree or determine these matters.

5 Nominated Subcontractors

5.1
Definition of "nominated Subcontractor"

In the Contract, "nominated Subcontractor" means a Subcontractor:

(a)   who is stated in the Contract as being a nominated Subcontractor, or

(b)   whom the Engineer, under Clause 13 [*Variations and Adjustments*], instructs the Contractor to employ as a Subcontractor.

5.2
Objection to Nomination

The Contractor shall not be under any obligation to employ a nominated Subcontractor against whom the Contractor raises reasonable objection by notice to the Engineer as soon as practicable, with supporting particulars. An objection shall be deemed reasonable if it arises from (among other things) any of the following matters, unless the Employer agrees to indemnify the Contractor against and from the consequences of the matter:

(a)   there are reasons to believe that the Subcontractor does not have sufficient competence, resources or financial strength;

(b)   the subcontract does not specify that the nominated Subcontractor shall indemnify the Contractor against and from any negligence or misuse of Goods by the nominated Subcontractor, his agents and employees; or

(c)   the subcontract does not specify that, for the subcontracted work (including design, if any), the nominated Subcontractor shall:

        (i)   undertake to the Contractor such obligations and liabilities as will enable the Contractor to discharge his obligations and liabilities under the Contract, and

        (ii)   indemnify the Contractor against and from all obligations and liabilities arising under or in connection with the Contract and from the consequences of any failure by the Subcontractor to perform these obligations or to fulfil these liabilities.

5.3
Payments to nominated Subcontractors

The Contractor shall pay to the nominated Subcontractor the amounts which the Engineer certifies to be due in accordance with the subcontract. These amounts plus other charges shall be included in the Contract Price in accordance with sub-paragraph (b) of Sub-Clause 13.5 [*Provisional Sums*], except as stated in Sub-Clause 5.4 [*Evidence of Payments*].

5.4
Evidence of Payments

Before issuing a Payment Certificate which includes an amount payable to a nominated Subcontractor, the Engineer may request the Contractor to supply reasonable evidence that the nominated Subcontractor has received all amounts due in accordance with previous Payment Certificates, less applicable deductions for retention or otherwise. Unless the Contractor:

(a)   submits this reasonable evidence to the Engineer, or

(b)   (i)   satisfies the Engineer in writing that the Contractor is reasonably entitled to withhold or refuse to pay these amounts, and

        (ii)   submits to the Engineer reasonable evidence that the nominated Subcontractor has been notified of the Contractor's entitlement,

then the Employer may (at his sole discretion) pay, direct to the nominated Subcontractor, part or all of such amounts previously certified (less applicable deductions) as are due to the nominated Subcontractor and for which the Contractor has failed to submit the evidence described in sub-paragraphs (a) or (b) above. The Contractor shall then repay, to the Employer, the amount which the nominated Sub-contractor was directly paid by the Employer.

6 Staff and Labour

6.1
Engagement of Staff and Labour

Except as otherwise stated in the Specification, the Contractor shall make arrangements for the engagement of all staff and labour, local or otherwise, and for their payment, housing, feeding and transport.

6.2
Rates of Wages and Conditions of Labour

The Contractor shall pay rates of wages, and observe conditions of labour, which are not lower than those established for the trade or industry where the work is carried out. If no established rates or conditions are applicable, the Contractor shall pay rates of wages and observe conditions which are not lower than the general level of wages and conditions observed locally by employers whose trade or industry is similar to that of the Contractor.

6.3
Persons in the Service of Employer

The Contractor shall not recruit, or attempt to recruit, staff and labour from amongst the Employer's Personnel.

6.4
Labour Laws

The Contractor shall comply with all the relevant labour Laws applicable to the Contractor's Personnel, including Laws relating to their employment, health, safety, welfare, immigration and emigration, and shall allow them all their legal rights.

The Contractor shall require his employees to obey all applicable Laws, including those concerning safety at work.

6.5
Working Hours

No work shall be carried out on the Site on locally recognised days of rest, or outside the normal working hours stated in the Appendix to Tender, unless:

(a)   otherwise stated in the Contract,
(b)   the Engineer gives consent, or
(c)   the work is unavoidable, or necessary for the protection of life or property or for the safety of the Works, in which case the Contractor shall immediately advise the Engineer.

6.6
Facilities for Staff and Labour

Except as otherwise stated in the Specification, the Contractor shall provide and maintain all necessary accommodation and welfare facilities for the Contractor's Personnel. The Contractor shall also provide facilities for the Employer's Personnel as stated in the Specification.

The Contractor shall not permit any of the Contractor's Personnel to maintain any temporary or permanent living quarters within the structures forming part of the Permanent Works.

6.7
Health and Safety

The Contractor shall at all times take all reasonable precautions to maintain the health and safety of the Contractor's Personnel. In collaboration with local health authorities,

Conditions of Contract for Construction

the Contractor shall ensure that medical staff, first aid facilities, sick bay and ambulance service are available at all times at the Site and at any accommodation for Contractor's and Employer's Personnel, and that suitable arrangements are made for all necessary welfare and hygiene requirements and for the prevention of epidemics.

The Contractor shall appoint an accident prevention officer at the Site, responsible for maintaining safety and protection against accidents. This person shall be qualified for this responsibility, and shall have the authority to issue instructions and take protective measures to prevent accidents. Throughout the execution of the Works, the Contractor shall provide whatever is required by this person to exercise this responsibility and authority.

The Contractor shall send, to the Engineer, details of any accident as soon as practicable after its occurrence. The Contractor shall maintain records and make reports concerning health, safety and welfare of persons, and damage to property, as the Engineer may reasonably require.

6.8
Contractor's Superintendence

Throughout the execution of the Works, and as long thereafter as is necessary to fulfil the Contractor's obligations, the Contractor shall provide all necessary superintendence to plan, arrange, direct, manage, inspect and test the work.

Superintendence shall be given by a sufficient number of persons having adequate knowledge of the language for communications (defined in Sub-Clause 1.4 [*Law and Language*]) and of the operations to be carried out (including the methods and techniques required, the hazards likely to be encountered and methods of preventing accidents), for the satisfactory and safe execution of the Works.

6.9
Contractor's Personnel

The Contractor's Personnel shall be appropriately qualified, skilled and experienced in their respective trades or occupations. The Engineer may require the Contractor to remove (or cause to be removed) any person employed on the Site or Works, including the Contractor's Representative if applicable, who:

(a)   persists in any misconduct or lack of care,
(b)   carries out duties incompetently or negligently,
(c)   fails to conform with any provisions of the Contract, or
(d)   persists in any conduct which is prejudicial to safety, health, or the protection of the environment.

If appropriate, the Contractor shall then appoint (or cause to be appointed) a suitable replacement person.

6.10
Records of Contractor's Personnel and Equipment

The Contractor shall submit, to the Engineer, details showing the number of each class of Contractor's Personnel and of each type of Contractor's Equipment on the Site. Details shall be submitted each calendar month, in a form approved by the Engineer, until the Contractor has completed all work which is known to be outstanding at the completion date stated in the Taking-Over Certificate for the Works.

6.11
Disorderly Conduct

The Contractor shall at all times take all reasonable precautions to prevent any unlawful, riotous or disorderly conduct by or amongst the Contractor's Personnel, and to preserve peace and protection of persons and property on and near the Site.

Plant, Materials and Workmanship

7.1

Manner of Execution

The Contractor shall carry out the manufacture of Plant, the production and manufacture of Materials, and all other execution of the Works:

(a)   in the manner (if any) specified in the Contract,

(b)   in a proper workmanlike and careful manner, in accordance with recognised good practice, and

(c)   with properly equipped facilities and non-hazardous Materials, except as otherwise specified in the Contract.

7.2

Samples

The Contractor shall submit the following samples of Materials, and relevant information, to the Engineer for consent prior to using the Materials in or for the Works:

(a)   manufacturer's standard samples of Materials and samples specified in the Contract, all at the Contractor's cost, and

(b)   additional samples instructed by the Engineer as a Variation.

Each sample shall be labelled as to origin and intended use in the Works.

7.3

Inspection

The Employer's Personnel shall at all reasonable times:

(a)   have full access to all parts of the Site and to all places from which natural Materials are being obtained, and

(b)   during production, manufacture and construction (at the Site and elsewhere), be entitled to examine, inspect, measure and test the materials and workmanship, and to check the progress of manufacture of Plant and production and manufacture of Materials.

The Contractor shall give the Employer's Personnel full opportunity to carry out these activities, including providing access, facilities, permissions and safety equipment. No such activity shall relieve the Contractor from any obligation or responsibility.

The Contractor shall give notice to the Engineer whenever any work is ready and before it is covered up, put out of sight, or packaged for storage or transport. The Engineer shall then either carry out the examination, inspection, measurement or testing without unreasonable delay, or promptly give notice to the Contractor that the Engineer does not require to do so. If the Contractor fails to give the notice, he shall, if and when required by the Engineer, uncover the work and thereafter reinstate and make good, all at the Contractor's cost.

7.4

Testing

This Sub-Clause shall apply to all tests specified in the Contract, other than the Tests after Completion (if any).

The Contractor shall provide all apparatus, assistance, documents and other information, electricity, equipment, fuel, consumables, instruments, labour, materials, and suitably qualified and experienced staff, as are necessary to carry out the specified tests efficiently. The Contractor shall agree, with the Engineer, the time and place for the specified testing of any Plant, Materials and other parts of the Works.

Conditions of Contract for Construction

The Engineer may, under Clause 13 [*Variations and Adjustments*], vary the location or details of specified tests, or instruct the Contractor to carry out additional tests. If these varied or additional tests show that the tested Plant, Materials or workmanship is not in accordance with the Contract, the cost of carrying out this Variation shall be borne by the Contractor, notwithstanding other provisions of the Contract.

The Engineer shall give the Contractor not less than 24 hours' notice of the Engineer's intention to attend the tests. If the Engineer does not attend at the time and place agreed, the Contractor may proceed with the tests, unless otherwise instructed by the Engineer, and the tests shall then be deemed to have been made in the Engineer's presence.

If the Contractor suffers delay and/or incurs Cost from complying with these instructions or as a result of a delay for which the Employer is responsible, the Contractor shall give notice to the Engineer and shall be entitled subject to Sub-Clause 20.1 [*Contractor's Claims*] to:

(a)   an extension of time for any such delay, if completion is or will be delayed, under Sub-Clause 8.4 [*Extension of Time for Completion*], and

(b)   payment of any such Cost plus reasonable profit, which shall be included in the Contract Price.

After receiving this notice, the Engineer shall proceed in accordance with Sub-Clause 3.5 [*Determinations*] to agree or determine these matters.

The Contractor shall promptly forward to the Engineer duly certified reports of the tests. When the specified tests have been passed, the Engineer shall endorse the Contractor's test certificate, or issue a certificate to him, to that effect. If the Engineer has not attended the tests, he shall be deemed to have accepted the readings as accurate.

7.5

Rejection

If, as a result of an examination, inspection, measurement or testing, any Plant, Materials or workmanship is found to be defective or otherwise not in accordance with the Contract, the Engineer may reject the Plant, Materials or workmanship by giving notice to the Contractor, with reasons. The Contractor shall then promptly make good the defect and ensure that the rejected item complies with the Contract.

If the Engineer requires this Plant, Materials or workmanship to be retested, the tests shall be repeated under the same terms and conditions. If the rejection and retesting cause the Employer to incur additional costs, the Contractor shall subject to Sub-Clause 2.5 [*Employer's Claims*] pay these costs to the Employer.

7.6

Remedial Work

Notwithstanding any previous test or certification, the Engineer may instruct the Contractor to:

(a)   remove from the Site and replace any Plant or Materials which is not in accordance with the Contract,

(b)   remove and re-execute any other work which is not in accordance with the Contract, and

(c)   execute any work which is urgently required for the safety of the Works, whether because of an accident, unforeseeable event or otherwise.

The Contractor shall comply with the instruction within a reasonable time, which shall be the time (if any) specified in the instruction, or immediately if urgency is specified under sub-paragraph (c).

If the Contractor fails to comply with the instruction, the Employer shall be entitled to employ and pay other persons to carry out the work. Except to the extent that the Contractor would have been entitled to payment for the work, the Contractor shall subject to Sub-Clause 2.5 [*Employer's Claims*] pay to the Employer all costs arising from this failure.

7.7

Ownership of Plant and Materials

Each item of Plant and Materials shall, to the extent consistent with the Laws of the Country, become the property of the Employer at whichever is the earlier of the following times, free from liens and other encumbrances:

(a)   when it is delivered to the Site;
(b)   when the Contractor is entitled to payment of the value of the Plant and Materials under Sub-Clause 8.10 [*Payment for Plant and Materials in Event of Suspension*].

7.8

Royalties

Unless otherwise stated in the Specification, the Contractor shall pay all royalties, rents and other payments for:

(a)   natural Materials obtained from outside the Site, and
(b)   the disposal of material from demolitions and excavations and of other surplus material (whether natural or man-made), except to the extent that disposal areas within the Site are specified in the Contract.

8 Commencement, Delays and Suspension

8.1
Commencement of Work

The Engineer shall give the Contractor not less than 7 days' notice of the Commencement Date. Unless otherwise stated in the Particular Conditions, the Commencement Date shall be within 42 days after the Contractor receives the Letter of Acceptance.

The Contractor shall commence the execution of the Works as soon as is reasonably practicable after the Commencement Date, and shall then proceed with the Works with due expedition and without delay.

8.2

Time for Completion

The Contractor shall complete the whole of the Works, and each Section (if any), within the Time for Completion for the Works or Section (as the case may be), including:

(a)   achieving the passing of the Tests on Completion, and
(b)   completing all work which is stated in the Contract as being required for the Works or Section to be considered to be completed for the purposes of taking-over under Sub-Clause 10.1 [*Taking Over of the Works and Sections*].

8.3

Programme

The Contractor shall submit a detailed time programme to the Engineer within 28 days after receiving the notice under Sub-Clause 8.1 [*Commencement of Works*]. The Contractor shall also submit a revised programme whenever the previous programme is inconsistent with actual progress or with the Contractor's obligations. Each programme shall include:

© FIDIC 1999

Conditions of Contract for Construction

(a)   the order in which the Contractor intends to carry out the Works, including the anticipated timing of each stage of design (if any), Contractor's Documents, procurement, manufacture of Plant, delivery to Site, construction, erection and testing,

(b)   each of these stages for work by each nominated Subcontractor (as defined in Clause 5 [*Nominated Subcontractors*]),

(c)   the sequence and timing of inspections and tests specified in the Contract, and

(d)   a supporting report which includes:

    (i)   a general description of the methods which the Contractor intends to adopt, and of the major stages, in the execution of the Works, and

    (ii)   details showing the Contractor's reasonable estimate of the number of each class of Contractor's Personnel and of each type of Contractor's Equipment, required on the Site for each major stage.

Unless the Engineer, within 21 days after receiving a programme, gives notice to the Contractor stating the extent to which it does not comply with the Contract, the Contractor shall proceed in accordance with the programme, subject to his other obligations under the Contract. The Employer's Personnel shall be entitled to rely upon the programme when planning their activities.

The Contractor shall promptly give notice to the Engineer of specific probable future events or circumstances which may adversely affect the work, increase the Contract Price or delay the execution of the Works. The Engineer may require the Contractor to submit an estimate of the anticipated effect of the future event or circumstances, and/or a proposal under Sub-Clause 13.3 [*Variation Procedure*].

If, at any time, the Engineer gives notice to the Contractor that a programme fails (to the extent stated) to comply with the Contract or to be consistent with actual progress and the Contractor's stated intentions, the Contractor shall submit a revised programme to the Engineer in accordance with this Sub-Clause.

8.4

Extension of Time for Completion

The Contractor shall be entitled subject to Sub-Clause 20.1 [*Contractor's Claims*] to an extension of the Time for Completion if and to the extent that completion for the purposes of Sub-Clause 10.1 [*Taking Over of the Works and Sections*] is or will be delayed by any of the following causes:

(a)   a Variation (unless an adjustment to the Time for Completion has been agreed under Sub-Clause 13.3 [*Variation Procedure*]) or other substantial change in the quantity of an item of work included in the Contract,

(b)   a cause of delay giving an entitlement to extension of time under a Sub-Clause of these Conditions,

(c)   exceptionally adverse climatic conditions,

(d)   Unforeseeable shortages in the availability of personnel or Goods caused by epidemic or governmental actions, or

(e)   any delay, impediment or prevention caused by or attributable to the Employer, the Employer's Personnel, or the Employer's other contractors on the Site.

If the Contractor considers himself to be entitled to an extension of the Time for Completion, the Contractor shall give notice to the Engineer in accordance with Sub-Clause 20.1 [*Contractor's Claims*]. When determining each extension of time under Sub-Clause 20.1, the Engineer shall review previous determinations and may increase, but shall not decrease, the total extension of time.

8.5
Delays Caused by
Authorities

If the following conditions apply, namely:

(a)   the Contractor has diligently followed the procedures laid down by the relevant legally constituted public authorities in the Country,

(b)   these authorities delay or disrupt the Contractor's work, and

(c)   the delay or disruption was Unforeseeable,

then this delay or disruption will be considered as a cause of delay under sub-paragraph (b) of Sub-Clause 8.4 [*Extension of Time for Completion*].

8.6
Rate of Progress

If, at any time:

(a)   actual progress is too slow to complete within the Time for Completion, and/or

(b)   progress has fallen (or will fall) behind the current programme under Sub-Clause 8.3 [*Programme*],

other than as a result of a cause listed in Sub-Clause 8.4 [*Extension of Time for Completion*], then the Engineer may instruct the Contractor to submit, under Sub-Clause 8.3 [*Programme*], a revised programme and supporting report describing the revised methods which the Contractor proposes to adopt in order to expedite progress and complete within the Time for Completion.

Unless the Engineer notifies otherwise, the Contractor shall adopt these revised methods, which may require increases in the working hours and/or in the numbers of Contractor's Personnel and/or Goods, at the risk and cost of the Contractor. If these revised methods cause the Employer to incur additional costs, the Contractor shall subject to Sub-Clause 2.5 [*Employer's Claims*] pay these costs to the Employer, in addition to delay damages (if any) under Sub-Clause 8.7 below.

8.7
Delay Damages

If the Contractor fails to comply with Sub-Clause 8.2 [*Time for Completion*], the Contractor shall subject to Sub-Clause 2.5 [*Employer's Claims*] pay delay damages to the Employer for this default. These delay damages shall be the sum stated in the Appendix to Tender, which shall be paid for every day which shall elapse between the relevant Time for Completion and the date stated in the Taking-Over Certificate. However, the total amount due under this Sub-Clause shall not exceed the maximum amount of delay damages (if any) stated in the Appendix to Tender.

These delay damages shall be the only damages due from the Contractor for such default, other than in the event of termination under Sub-Clause 15.2 [*Termination by Employer*] prior to completion of the Works. These damages shall not relieve the Contractor from his obligation to complete the Works, or from any other duties, obligations or responsibilities which he may have under the Contract.

8.8
Suspension of Work

The Engineer may at any time instruct the Contractor to suspend progress of part or all of the Works. During such suspension, the Contractor shall protect, store and secure such part or the Works against any deterioration, loss or damage.

The Engineer may also notify the cause for the suspension. If and to the extent that the cause is notified and is the responsibility of the Contractor, the following Sub-Clauses 8.9, 8.10 and 8.11 shall not apply.

Conditions of Contract for Construction

| 8.9 | If the Contractor suffers delay and/or incurs Cost from complying with the Engineer's |
| Consequences of Suspension | instructions under Sub-Clause 8.8 [*Suspension of Work*] and/or from resuming the work, the Contractor shall give notice to the Engineer and shall be entitled subject to Sub-Clause 20.1 [*Contractor's Claims*] to: |

(a)   an extension of time for any such delay, if completion is or will be delayed, under Sub-Clause 8.4 [*Extension of Time for Completion*], and

(b)   payment of any such Cost, which shall be included in the Contract Price.

After receiving this notice, the Engineer shall proceed in accordance with Sub-Clause 3.5 [*Determinations*] to agree or determine these matters.

The Contractor shall not be entitled to an extension of time for, or to payment of the Cost incurred in, making good the consequences of the Contractor's faulty design, workmanship or materials, or of the Contractor's failure to protect, store or secure in accordance with Sub-Clause 8.8 [*Suspension of Work*].

8.10

Payment for Plant and Materials in Event of Suspension

The Contractor shall be entitled to payment of the value (as at the date of suspension) of Plant and/or Materials which have not been delivered to Site, if:

(a)   the work on Plant or delivery of Plant and/or Materials has been suspended for more than 28 days, and

(b)   the Contractor has marked the Plant and/or Materials as the Employer's property in accordance with the Engineer's instructions.

8.11

Prolonged Suspension

If the suspension under Sub-Clause 8.8 [*Suspension of Work*] has continued for more than 84 days, the Contractor may request the Engineer's permission to proceed. If the Engineer does not give permission within 28 days after being requested to do so, the Contractor may, by giving notice to the Engineer, treat the suspension as an omission under Clause 13 [*Variations and Adjustments*] of the affected part of the Works. If the suspension affects the whole of the Works, the Contractor may give notice of termination under Sub-Clause 16.2 [*Termination by Contractor*].

8.12

Resumption of Work

After the permission or instruction to proceed is given, the Contractor and the Engineer shall jointly examine the Works and the Plant and Materials affected by the suspension. The Contractor shall make good any deterioration or defect in or loss of the Works or Plant or Materials, which has occurred during the suspension.

Tests 9 on Completion

9.1

Contractor's Obligations

The Contractor shall carry out the Tests on Completion in accordance with this Clause and Sub-Clause 7.4 [*Testing*], after providing the documents in accordance with sub-paragraph (d) of Sub-Clause 4.1 [*Contractor's General Obligations*].

The Contractor shall give to the Engineer not less than 21 days' notice of the date after which the Contractor will be ready to carry out each of the Tests on Completion. Unless otherwise agreed, Tests on Completion shall be carried out within 14 days after this date, on such day or days as the Engineer shall instruct.

In considering the results of the Tests on Completion, the Engineer shall make allowances for the effect of any use of the Works by the Employer on the performance or other characteristics of the Works. As soon as the Works, or a Section, have passed any Tests on Completion, the Contractor shall submit a certified report of the results of these Tests to the Engineer.

9.2

Delayed Tests

If the Tests on Completion are being unduly delayed by the Employer, Sub-Clause 7.4 [*Testing*] (fifth paragraph) and/or Sub-Clause 10.3 [*Interference with Tests on Completion*] shall be applicable.

If the Tests on Completion are being unduly delayed by the Contractor, the Engineer may by notice require the Contractor to carry out the Tests within 21 days after receiving the notice. The Contractor shall carry out the Tests on such day or days within that period as the Contractor may fix and of which he shall give notice to the Engineer.

If the Contractor fails to carry out the Tests on Completion within the period of 21 days, the Employer's Personnel may proceed with the Tests at the risk and cost of the Contractor. The Tests on Completion shall then be deemed to have been carried out in the presence of the Contractor and the results of the Tests shall be accepted as accurate.

9.3

Retesting

If the Works, or a Section, fail to pass the Tests on Completion, Sub-Clause 7.5 [*Rejection*] shall apply, and the Engineer or the Contractor may require the failed Tests, and Tests on Completion on any related work, to be repeated under the same terms and conditions.

9.4

Failure to Pass Tests on Completion

If the Works, or a Section, fail to pass the Tests on Completion repeated under Sub-Clause 9.3 [*Retesting*], the Engineer shall be entitled to:

(a)   order further repetition of Tests on Completion under Sub-Clause 9.3;

(b)   if the failure deprives the Employer of substantially the whole benefit of the Works or Section, reject the Works or Section (as the case may be), in which event the Employer shall have the same remedies as are provided in sub-paragraph (c) of Sub-Clause 11.4 [*Failure to Remedy Defects*]; or

(c)   issue a Taking-Over Certificate, if the Employer so requests.

In the event of sub-paragraph (c), the Contractor shall proceed in accordance with all other obligations under the Contract, and the Contract Price shall be reduced by such amount as shall be appropriate to cover the reduced value to the Employer as a result of this failure. Unless the relevant reduction for this failure is stated (or its method of calculation is defined) in the Contract, the Employer may require the reduction to be (i) agreed by both Parties (in full satisfaction of this failure only) and paid before this Taking-Over Certificate is issued, or (ii) determined and paid under Sub-Clause 2.5 [*Employer's Claims*] and Sub-Clause 3.5 [*Determinations*].

10 Employer's Taking Over

10.1

Taking Over of the Works and Sections

Except as stated in Sub-Clause 9.4 [*Failure to Pass Tests on Completion*], the Works shall be taken over by the Employer when (i) the Works have been completed in accordance with the Contract, including the matters described in Sub-Clause 8.2 [*Time for Completion*] and except as allowed in sub-paragraph (a) below, and (ii) a

Taking-Over Certificate for the Works has been issued, or is deemed to have been issued in accordance with this Sub-Clause.

The Contractor may apply by notice to the Engineer for a Taking-Over Certificate not earlier than 14 days before the Works will, in the Contractor's opinion, be complete and ready for taking over. If the Works are divided into Sections, the Contractor may similarly apply for a Taking-Over Certificate for each Section.

The Engineer shall, within 28 days after receiving the Contractor's application:

(a)   issue the Taking-Over Certificate to the Contractor, stating the date on which the Works or Section were completed in accordance with the Contract, except for any minor outstanding work and defects which will not substantially affect the use of the Works or Section for their intended purpose (either until or whilst this work is completed and these defects are remedied); or

(b)   reject the application, giving reasons and specifying the work required to be done by the Contractor to enable the Taking-Over Certificate to be issued. The Contractor shall then complete this work before issuing a further notice under this Sub-Clause.

If the Engineer fails either to issue the Taking-Over Certificate or to reject the Contractor's application within the period of 28 days, and if the Works or Section (as the case may be) are substantially in accordance with the Contract, the Taking-Over Certificate shall be deemed to have been issued on the last day of that period.

10.2

**Taking Over
of Parts of the Works**

The Engineer may, at the sole discretion of the Employer, issue a Taking-Over Certificate for any part of the Permanent Works.

The Employer shall not use any part of the Works (other than as a temporary measure which is either specified in the Contract or agreed by both Parties) unless and until the Engineer has issued a Taking-Over Certificate for this part. However, if the Employer does use any part of the Works before the Taking-Over Certificate is issued:

(a)   the part which is used shall be deemed to have been taken over as from the date on which it is used,

(b)   the Contractor shall cease to be liable for the care of such part as from this date, when responsibility shall pass to the Employer, and

(c)   if requested by the Contractor, the Engineer shall issue a Taking-Over Certificate for this part.

After the Engineer has issued a Taking-Over Certificate for a part of the Works, the Contractor shall be given the earliest opportunity to take such steps as may be necessary to carry out any outstanding Tests on Completion. The Contractor shall carry out these Tests on Completion as soon as practicable before the expiry date of the relevant Defects Notification Period.

If the Contractor incurs Cost as a result of the Employer taking over and/or using a part of the Works, other than such use as is specified in the Contract or agreed by the Contractor, the Contractor shall (i) give notice to the Engineer and (ii) be entitled subject to Sub-Clause 20.1 [*Contractor's Claims*] to payment of any such Cost plus reasonable profit, which shall be included in the Contract Price. After receiving this notice, the Engineer shall proceed in accordance with Sub-Clause 3.5 [*Determinations*] to agree or determine this Cost and profit.

If a Taking-Over Certificate has been issued for a part of the Works (other than a Section), the delay damages thereafter for completion of the remainder of the Works shall be reduced. Similarly, the delay damages for the remainder of the Section (if any) in which this part is included shall also be reduced. For any period of delay after the date stated in this Taking-Over Certificate, the proportional reduction in these delay damages shall be calculated as the proportion which the value of the part so certified bears to the value of the Works or Section (as the case may be) as a whole. The Engineer shall proceed in accordance with Sub-Clause 3.5 [Determinations] to agree or determine these proportions. The provisions of this paragraph shall only apply to the daily rate of delay damages under Sub-Clause 8.7 [Delay Damages], and shall not affect the maximum amount of these damages.

10.3

Interference with Tests on Completion

If the Contractor is prevented, for more than 14 days, from carrying out the Tests on Completion by a cause for which the Employer is responsible, the Employer shall be deemed to have taken over the Works or Section (as the case may be) on the date when the Tests on Completion would otherwise have been completed.

The Engineer shall then issue a Taking-Over Certificate accordingly, and the Contractor shall carry out the Tests on Completion as soon as practicable, before the expiry date of the Defects Notification Period. The Engineer shall require the Tests on Completion to be carried out by giving 14 days' notice and in accordance with the relevant provisions of the Contract.

If the Contractor suffers delay and/or incurs Cost as a result of this delay in carrying out the Tests on Completion, the Contractor shall give notice to the Engineer and shall be entitled subject to Sub-Clause 20.1 [Contractor's Claims] to:

(a)   an extension of time for any such delay, if completion is or will be delayed, under Sub-Clause 8.4 [Extension of Time for Completion], and

(b)   payment of any such Cost plus reasonable profit, which shall be included in the Contract Price.

After receiving this notice, the Engineer shall proceed in accordance with Sub-Clause 3.5 [Determinations] to agree or determine these matters.

10.4

Surfaces Requiring Reinstatement

Except as otherwise stated in a Taking-Over Certificate, a certificate for a Section or part of the Works shall not be deemed to certify completion of any ground or other surfaces requiring reinstatement.

11 Defects Liability

11.1

Completion of Outstanding Work and Remedying Defects

In order that the Works and Contractor's Documents, and each Section, shall be in the condition required by the Contract (fair wear and tear excepted) by the expiry date of the relevant Defects Notification Period or as soon as practicable thereafter, the Contractor shall:

(a)   complete any work which is outstanding on the date stated in a Taking-Over Certificate, within such reasonable time as is instructed by the Engineer, and

(b)   execute all work required to remedy defects or damage, as may be notified by (or on behalf of) the Employer on or before the expiry date of the Defects Notification Period for the Works or Section (as the case may be).

If a defect appears or damage occurs, the Contractor shall be notified accordingly, by (or on behalf of) the Employer.

11.2

Cost of Remedying Defects

All work referred to in sub-paragraph (b) of Sub-Clause 11.1 [*Completion of Outstanding Work and Remedying Defects*] shall be executed at the risk and cost of the Contractor, if and to the extent that the work is attributable to:

(a) any design for which the Contractor is responsible,
(b) Plant, Materials or workmanship not being in accordance with the Contract, or
(c) failure by the Contractor to comply with any other obligation.

If and to the extent that such work is attributable to any other cause, the Contractor shall be notified promptly by (or on behalf of) the Employer, and Sub-Clause 13.3 [*Variation Procedure*] shall apply.

11.3

Extension of Defects Notification Period

The Employer shall be entitled subject to Sub-Clause 2.5 [*Employer's Claims*] to an extension of the Defects Notification Period for the Works or a Section if and to the extent that the Works, Section or a major item of Plant (as the case may be, and after taking over) cannot be used for the purposes for which they are intended by reason of a defect or damage. However, a Defects Notification Period shall not be extended by more than two years.

If delivery and/or erection of Plant and/or Materials was suspended under Sub-Clause 8.8 [*Suspension of Work*] or Sub-Clause 16.1 [*Contractor's Entitlement to Suspend Work*], the Contractor's obligations under this Clause shall not apply to any defects or damage occurring more than two years after the Defects Notification Period for the Plant and/or Materials would otherwise have expired.

11.4

Failure to Remedy Defects

If the Contractor fails to remedy any defect or damage within a reasonable time, a date may be fixed by (or on behalf of) the Employer, on or by which the defect or damage is to be remedied. The Contractor shall be given reasonable notice of this date.

If the Contractor fails to remedy the defect or damage by this notified date and this remedial work was to be executed at the cost of the Contractor under Sub-Clause 11.2 [*Cost of Remedying Defects*], the Employer may (at his option):

(a) carry out the work himself or by others, in a reasonable manner and at the Contractor's cost, but the Contractor shall have no responsibility for this work; and the Contractor shall subject to Sub-Clause 2.5 [*Employer's Claims*] pay to the Employer the costs reasonably incurred by the Employer in remedying the defect or damage;
(b) require the Engineer to agree or determine a reasonable reduction in the Contract Price in accordance with Sub-Clause 3.5 [*Determinations*]; or
(c) if the defect or damage deprives the Employer of substantially the whole benefit of the Works or any major part of the Works, terminate the Contract as a whole, or in respect of such major part which cannot be put to the intended use. Without prejudice to any other rights, under the Contract or otherwise, the Employer shall then be entitled to recover all sums paid for the Works or for such part (as the case may be), plus financing costs and the cost of dismantling the same, clearing the Site and returning Plant and Materials to the Contractor.

11.5

Removal of Defective Work

If the defect or damage cannot be remedied expeditiously on the Site and the Employer gives consent, the Contractor may remove from the Site for the purposes of repair such items of Plant as are defective or damaged. This consent may require the Contractor to increase the amount of the Performance Security by the full replacement cost of these items, or to provide other appropriate security.

11.6

Further Tests

If the work of remedying of any defect or damage may affect the performance of the Works, the Engineer may require the repetition of any of the tests described in the Contract. The requirement shall be made by notice within 28 days after the defect or damage is remedied.

These tests shall be carried out in accordance with the terms applicable to the previous tests, except that they shall be carried out at the risk and cost of the Party liable, under Sub-Clause 11.2 [*Cost of Remedying Defects*], for the cost of the remedial work.

11.7

Right of Access

Until the Performance Certificate has been issued, the Contractor shall have such right of access to the Works as is reasonably required in order to comply with this Clause, except as may be inconsistent with the Employer's reasonable security restrictions.

11.8

Contractor to Search

The Contractor shall, if required by the Engineer, search for the cause of any defect, under the direction of the Engineer. Unless the defect is to be remedied at the cost of the Contractor under Sub-Clause 11.2 [*Cost of Remedying Defects*], the Cost of the search plus reasonable profit shall be agreed or determined by the Engineer in accordance with Sub-Clause 3.5 [*Determinations*] and shall be included in the Contract Price.

11.9

Performance Certificate

Performance of the Contractor's obligations shall not be considered to have been completed until the Engineer has issued the Performance Certificate to the Contractor, stating the date on which the Contractor completed his obligations under the Contract.

The Engineer shall issue the Performance Certificate within 28 days after the latest of the expiry dates of the Defects Notification Periods, or as soon thereafter as the Contractor has supplied all the Contractor's Documents and completed and tested all the Works, including remedying any defects. A copy of the Performance Certificate shall be issued to the Employer.

Only the Performance Certificate shall be deemed to constitute acceptance of the Works.

11.10

Unfulfilled Obligations

After the Performance Certificate has been issued, each Party shall remain liable for the fulfilment of any obligation which remains unperformed at that time. For the purposes of determining the nature and extent of unperformed obligations, the Contract shall be deemed to remain in force.

11.11

Clearance of Site

Upon receiving the Performance Certificate, the Contractor shall remove any remaining Contractor's Equipment, surplus material, wreckage, rubbish and Temporary Works from the Site.

If all these items have not been removed within 28 days after the Employer receives a copy of the Performance Certificate, the Employer may sell or

© FIDIC 1999   Conditions of Contract for Construction

otherwise dispose of any remaining items. The Employer shall be entitled to be paid the costs incurred in connection with, or attributable to, such sale or disposal and restoring the Site.

Any balance of the moneys from the sale shall be paid to the Contractor. If these moneys are less than the Employer's costs, the Contractor shall pay the outstanding balance to the Employer.

12 Measurement and Evaluation

12.1

Works to be Measured

The Works shall be measured, and valued for payment, in accordance with this Clause.

Whenever the Engineer requires any part of the Works to be measured, reasonable notice shall be given to the Contractor's Representative, who shall:

(a)   promptly either attend or send another qualified representative to assist the Engineer in making the measurement, and

(b)   supply any particulars requested by the Engineer.

If the Contractor fails to attend or send a representative, the measurement made by (or on behalf of) the Engineer shall be accepted as accurate.

Except as otherwise stated in the Contract, wherever any Permanent Works are to be measured from records, these shall be prepared by the Engineer. The Contractor shall, as and when requested, attend to examine and agree the records with the Engineer, and shall sign the same when agreed. If the Contractor does not attend, the records shall be accepted as accurate.

If the Contractor examines and disagrees with the records, and/or does not sign them as agreed, then the Contractor shall give notice to the Engineer of the respects in which the records are asserted to be inaccurate. After receiving this notice, the Engineer shall review the records and either confirm or vary them. If the Contractor does not so give notice to the Engineer within 14 days after being requested to examine the records, they shall be accepted as accurate.

12.2

Method of Measurement

Except as otherwise stated in the Contract and notwithstanding local practice:

(a)   measurement shall be made of the net actual quantity of each item of the Permanent Works, and

(b)   the method of measurement shall be in accordance with the Bill of Quantities or other applicable Schedules.

12.3

Evaluation

Except as otherwise stated in the Contract, the Engineer shall proceed in accordance with Sub-Clause 3.5 [*Determinations*] to agree or determine the Contract Price by evaluating each item of work, applying the measurement agreed or determined in accordance with the above Sub-Clauses 12.1 and 12.2 and the appropriate rate or price for the item.

For each item of work, the appropriate rate or price for the item shall be the rate or price specified for such item in the Contract or, if there is no such item, specified for similar work. However, a new rate or price shall be appropriate for an item of work if:

(a)   (i)   the measured quantity of the item is changed by more than 10% from the quantity of this item in the Bill of Quantities or other Schedule,

       (ii)   this change in quantity multiplied by such specified rate for this item exceeds 0.01% of the Accepted Contract Amount,

       (iii) this change in quantity directly changes the Cost per unit quantity of this item by more than 1%, and

       (iv) this item is not specified in the Contract as a "fixed rate item";

or

(b)   (i)   the work is instructed under Clause 13 [*Variations and Adjustments*],

       (ii)   no rate or price is specified in the Contract for this item, and

       (iii) no specified rate or price is appropriate because the item of work is not of similar character, or is not executed under similar conditions, as any item in the Contract.

Each new rate or price shall be derived from any relevant rates or prices in the Contract, with reasonable adjustments to take account of the matters described in sub-paragraph (a) and/or (b), as applicable. If no rates or prices are relevant for the derivation of a new rate or price, it shall be derived from the reasonable Cost of executing the work, together with reasonable profit, taking account of any other relevant matters.

Until such time as an appropriate rate or price is agreed or determined, the Engineer shall determine a provisional rate or price for the purposes of Interim Payment Certificates.

12.4
Omissions

Whenever the omission of any work forms part (or all) of a Variation, the value of which has not been agreed, if:

(a)   the Contractor will incur (or has incurred) cost which, if the work had not been omitted, would have been deemed to be covered by a sum forming part of the Accepted Contract Amount;

(b)   the omission of the work will result (or has resulted) in this sum not forming part of the Contract Price; and

(c)   this cost is not deemed to be included in the evaluation of any substituted work;

then the Contractor shall give notice to the Engineer accordingly, with supporting particulars. Upon receiving this notice, the Engineer shall proceed in accordance with Sub-Clause 3.5 [*Determinations*] to agree or determine this cost, which shall be included in the Contract Price.

13 Variations and Adjustments

13.1
Right to Vary

Variations may be initiated by the Engineer at any time prior to issuing the Taking-Over Certificate for the Works, either by an instruction or by a request for the Contractor to submit a proposal.

The Contractor shall execute and be bound by each Variation, unless the Contractor promptly gives notice to the Engineer stating (with supporting particulars) that the Contractor cannot readily obtain the Goods required for the Variation. Upon receiving this notice, the Engineer shall cancel, confirm or vary the instruction.

Each Variation may include:

© FIDIC 1999

Conditions of Contract for Construction

(a)   changes to the quantities of any item of work included in the Contract (however, such changes do not necessarily constitute a Variation),

(b)   changes to the quality and other characteristics of any item of work,

(c)   changes to the levels, positions and/or dimensions of any part of the Works,

(d)   omission of any work unless it is to be carried out by others,

(e)   any additional work, Plant, Materials or services necessary for the Permanent Works, including any associated Tests on Completion, boreholes and other testing and exploratory work, or

(f)   changes to the sequence or timing of the execution of the Works.

The Contractor shall not make any alteration and/or modification of the Permanent Works, unless and until the Engineer instructs or approves a Variation.

13.2

Value Engineering

The Contractor may, at any time, submit to the Engineer a written proposal which (in the Contractor's opinion) will, if adopted, (i) accelerate completion, (ii) reduce the cost to the Employer of executing, maintaining or operating the Works, (iii) improve the efficiency or value to the Employer of the completed Works, or (iv) otherwise be of benefit to the Employer.

The proposal shall be prepared at the cost of the Contractor and shall include the items listed in Sub-Clause 13.3 [*Variation Procedure*].

If a proposal, which is approved by the Engineer, includes a change in the design of part of the Permanent Works, then unless otherwise agreed by both Parties:

(a)   the Contractor shall design this part,

(b)   sub-paragraphs (a) to (d) of Sub-Clause 4.1 [*Contractor's General Obligations*] shall apply, and

(c)   if this change results in a reduction in the contract value of this part, the Engineer shall proceed in accordance with Sub-Clause 3.5 [*Determinations*] to agree or determine a fee, which shall be included in the Contract Price. This fee shall be half (50%) of the difference between the following amounts:

(i)   such reduction in contract value, resulting from the change, excluding adjustments under Sub-Clause 13.7 [*Adjustments for Changes in Legislation*] and Sub-Clause 13.8 [*Adjustments for Changes in Cost*], and

(ii)   the reduction (if any) in the value to the Employer of the varied works, taking account of any reductions in quality, anticipated life or operational efficiencies.

However, if amount (i) is less than amount (ii), there shall not be a fee.

13.3

Variation Procedure

If the Engineer requests a proposal, prior to instructing a Variation, the Contractor shall respond in writing as soon as practicable, either by giving reasons why he cannot comply (if this is the case) or by submitting:

(a)   a description of the proposed work to be performed and a programme for its execution,

(b)   the Contractor's proposal for any necessary modifications to the programme according to Sub-Clause 8.3 [*Programme*] and to the Time for Completion, and

(c)   the Contractor's proposal for evaluation of the Variation.

The Engineer shall, as soon as practicable after receiving such proposal (under Sub-Clause 13.2 [*Value Engineering*] or otherwise), respond with approval, disapproval or comments. The Contractor shall not delay any work whilst awaiting a response.

Each instruction to execute a Variation, with any requirements for the recording of Costs, shall be issued by the Engineer to the Contractor, who shall acknowledge receipt.

Each Variation shall be evaluated in accordance with Clause 12 [*Measurement and Evaluation*], unless the Engineer instructs or approves otherwise in accordance with this Clause.

13.4

Payment in Applicable Currencies

If the Contract provides for payment of the Contract Price in more than one currency, then whenever an adjustment is agreed, approved or determined as stated above, the amount payable in each of the applicable currencies shall be specified. For this purpose, reference shall be made to the actual or expected currency proportions of the Cost of the varied work, and to the proportions of various currencies specified for payment of the Contract Price.

13.5

Provisional Sums

Each Provisional Sum shall only be used, in whole or in part, in accordance with the Engineer's instructions, and the Contract Price shall be adjusted accordingly. The total sum paid to the Contractor shall include only such amounts, for the work, supplies or services to which the Provisional Sum relates, as the Engineer shall have instructed. For each Provisional Sum, the Engineer may instruct:

(a)   work to be executed (including Plant, Materials or services to be supplied) by the Contractor and valued under Sub-Clause 13.3 [*Variation Procedure*]; and/or

(b)   Plant, Materials or services to be purchased by the Contractor, from a nominated Subcontractor (as defined in Clause 5 [*Nominated Subcontractors*]) or otherwise; and for which there shall be included in the Contract Price:

(i)   the actual amounts paid (or due to be paid) by the Contractor, and

(ii)   a sum for overhead charges and profit, calculated as a percentage of these actual amounts by applying the relevant percentage rate (if any) stated in the appropriate Schedule. If there is no such rate, the percentage rate stated in the Appendix to Tender shall be applied.

The Contractor shall, when required by the Engineer, produce quotations, invoices, vouchers and accounts or receipts in substantiation.

13.6

Daywork

For work of a minor or incidental nature, the Engineer may instruct that a Variation shall be executed on a daywork basis. The work shall then be valued in accordance with the Daywork Schedule included in the Contract, and the following procedure shall apply. If a Daywork Schedule is not included in the Contract, this Sub-Clause shall not apply.

Before ordering Goods for the work, the Contractor shall submit quotations to the Engineer. When applying for payment, the Contractor shall submit invoices, vouchers and accounts or receipts for any Goods.

Except for any items for which the Daywork Schedule specifies that payment is not due, the Contractor shall deliver each day to the Engineer accurate statements in duplicate which shall include the following details of the resources used in executing the previous day's work:

(a)   the names, occupations and time of Contractor's Personnel,

(b)   the identification, type and time of Contractor's Equipment and Temporary Works, and

(c)   the quantities and types of Plant and Materials used.

One copy of each statement will, if correct, or when agreed, be signed by the Engineer and returned to the Contractor. The Contractor shall then submit priced statements of these resources to the Engineer, prior to their inclusion in the next Statement under Sub-Clause 14.3 [*Application for Interim Payment Certificates*].

13.7

Adjustments for Changes in Legislation

The Contract Price shall be adjusted to take account of any increase or decrease in Cost resulting from a change in the Laws of the Country (including the introduction of new Laws and the repeal or modification of existing Laws) or in the judicial or official governmental interpretation of such Laws, made after the Base Date, which affect the Contractor in the performance of obligations under the Contract.

If the Contractor suffers (or will suffer) delay and/or incurs (or will incur) additional Cost as a result of these changes in the Laws or in such interpretations, made after the Base Date, the Contractor shall give notice to the Engineer and shall be entitled subject to Sub-Clause 20.1 [*Contractor's Claims*] to:

(a)   an extension of time for any such delay, if completion is or will be delayed, under Sub-Clause 8.4 [*Extension of Time for Completion*], and

(b)   payment of any such Cost, which shall be included in the Contract Price.

After receiving this notice, the Engineer shall proceed in accordance with Sub-Clause 3.5 [*Determinations*] to agree or determine these matters.

13.8

Adjustments for Changes in Cost

In this Sub-Clause, "table of adjustment data" means the completed table of adjustment data included in the Appendix to Tender. If there is no such table of adjustment data, this Sub-Clause shall not apply.

If this Sub-Clause applies, the amounts payable to the Contractor shall be adjusted for rises or falls in the cost of labour, Goods and other inputs to the Works, by the addition or deduction of the amounts determined by the formulae prescribed in this Sub-Clause. To the extent that full compensation for any rise or fall in Costs is not covered by the provisions of this or other Clauses, the Accepted Contract Amount shall be deemed to have included amounts to cover the contingency of other rises and falls in costs.

The adjustment to be applied to the amount otherwise payable to the Contractor, as valued in accordance with the appropriate Schedule and certified in Payment Certificates, shall be determined from formulae for each of the currencies in which the Contract Price is payable. No adjustment is to be applied to work valued on the basis of Cost or current prices. The formulae shall be of the following general type:

$$P_n = a + b\frac{L_n}{L_o} + c\frac{E_n}{E_o} + d\frac{M_n}{M_o} + \ldots\ldots$$

where:

"P_n" is the adjustment multiplier to be applied to the estimated contract value in the relevant currency of the work carried out in period "n", this period being a month unless otherwise stated in the Appendix to Tender;

"a" is a fixed coefficient, stated in the relevant table of adjustment data, representing the non-adjustable portion in contractual payments;

"b", "c", "d", ... are coefficients representing the estimated proportion of each cost element related to the execution of the Works, as stated in the relevant table of adjustment data; such tabulated cost elements may be indicative of resources such as labour, equipment and materials;

"L_n", "E_n", "M_n", … are the current cost indices or reference prices for period "n", expressed in the relevant currency of payment, each of which is applicable to the relevant tabulated cost element on the date 49 days prior to the last day of the period (to which the particular Payment Certificate relates); and

"L_o", "E_o", "M_o", … are the base cost indices or reference prices, expressed in the relevant currency of payment, each of which is applicable to the relevant tabulated cost element on the Base Date.

The cost indices or reference prices stated in the table of adjustment data shall be used. If their source is in doubt, it shall be determined by the Engineer. For this purpose, reference shall be made to the values of the indices at stated dates (quoted in the fourth and fifth columns respectively of the table) for the purposes of clarification of the source; although these dates (and thus these values) may not correspond to the base cost indices.

In cases where the "currency of index" (stated in the table) is not the relevant currency of payment, each index shall be converted into the relevant currency of payment at the selling rate, established by the central bank of the Country, of this relevant currency on the above date for which the index is required to be applicable.

Until such time as each current cost index is available, the Engineer shall determine a provisional index for the issue of Interim Payment Certificates. When a current cost index is available, the adjustment shall be recalculated accordingly.

If the Contractor fails to complete the Works within the Time for Completion, adjustment of prices thereafter shall be made using either (i) each index or price applicable on the date 49 days prior to the expiry of the Time for Completion of the Works, or (ii) the current index or price: whichever is more favourable to the Employer.

The weightings (coefficients) for each of the factors of cost stated in the table(s) of adjustment data shall only be adjusted if they have been rendered unreasonable, unbalanced or inapplicable, as a result of Variations.

Contract Price and Payment

14.1

The Contract Price

Unless otherwise stated in the Particular Conditions:

(a) the Contract Price shall be agreed or determined under Sub-Clause 12.3 [*Evaluation*] and be subject to adjustments in accordance with the Contract;

(b) the Contractor shall pay all taxes, duties and fees required to be paid by him under the Contract, and the Contract Price shall not be adjusted for any of these costs except as stated in Sub-Clause 13.7 [*Adjustments for Changes in Legislation*];

(c) any quantities which may be set out in the Bill of Quantities or other Schedule are estimated quantities and are not to be taken as the actual and correct quantities:

(i) of the Works which the Contractor is required to execute, or
(ii) for the purposes of Clause 12 [*Measurement and Evaluation*]; and

(d) the Contractor shall submit to the Engineer, within 28 days after the Commencement Date, a proposed breakdown of each lump sum price in the Schedules. The Engineer may take account of the breakdown when preparing Payment Certificates, but shall not be bound by it.

14.2

Advance Payment

The Employer shall make an advance payment, as an interest-free loan for mobilisation, when the Contractor submits a guarantee in accordance with this Sub-Clause. The total advance payment, the number and timing of instalments (if more than one), and the applicable currencies and proportions, shall be as stated in the Appendix to Tender.

Unless and until the Employer receives this guarantee, or if the total advance payment is not stated in the Appendix to Tender, this Sub-Clause shall not apply.

The Engineer shall issue an Interim Payment Certificate for the first instalment after receiving a Statement (under Sub-Clause 14.3 [*Application for Interim Payment Certificates*]) and after the Employer receives (i) the Performance Security in accordance with Sub-Clause 4.2 [*Performance Security*] and (ii) a guarantee in amounts and currencies equal to the advance payment. This guarantee shall be issued by an entity and from within a country (or other jurisdiction) approved by the Employer, and shall be in the form annexed to the Particular Conditions or in another form approved by the Employer.

The Contractor shall ensure that the guarantee is valid and enforceable until the advance payment has been repaid, but its amount may be progressively reduced by the amount repaid by the Contractor as indicated in the Payment Certificates. If the terms of the guarantee specify its expiry date, and the advance payment has not been repaid by the date 28 days prior to the expiry date, the Contractor shall extend the validity of the guarantee until the advance payment has been repaid.

The advance payment shall be repaid through percentage deductions in Payment Certificates. Unless other percentages are stated in the Appendix to Tender:

(a) deductions shall commence in the Payment Certificate in which the total of all certified interim payments (excluding the advance payment and deductions and repayments of retention) exceeds ten per cent (10%) of the Accepted Contract Amount less Provisional Sums; and

(b) deductions shall be made at the amortisation rate of one quarter (25%) of the amount of each Payment Certificate (excluding the advance payment and deductions and repayments of retention) in the currencies and proportions of the advance payment, until such time as the advance payment has been repaid.

If the advance payment has not been repaid prior to the issue of the Taking-Over Certificate for the Works or prior to termination under Clause 15 [*Termination by Employer*], Clause 16 [*Suspension and Termination by Contractor*] or Clause 19 [*Force Majeure*] (as the case may be), the whole of the balance then outstanding shall immediately become due and payable by the Contractor to the Employer.

14.3

Application for Interim Payment Certificates

The Contractor shall submit a Statement in six copies to the Engineer after the end of each month, in a form approved by the Engineer, showing in detail the amounts to which the Contractor considers himself to be entitled, together with supporting documents which shall include the report on the progress during this month in accordance with Sub-Clause 4.21 [*Progress Reports*].

The Statement shall include the following items, as applicable, which shall be expressed in the various currencies in which the Contract Price is payable, in the sequence listed:

(a)   the estimated contract value of the Works executed and the Contractor's Documents produced up to the end of the month (including Variations but excluding items described in sub-paragraphs (b) to (g) below);

(b)   any amounts to be added and deducted for changes in legislation and changes in cost, in accordance with Sub-Clause 13.7 [*Adjustments for Changes in Legislation*] and Sub-Clause 13.8 [*Adjustments for Changes in Cost*];

(c)   any amount to be deducted for retention, calculated by applying the percentage of retention stated in the Appendix to Tender to the total of the above amounts, until the amount so retained by the Employer reaches the limit of Retention Money (if any) stated in the Appendix to Tender;

(d)   any amounts to be added and deducted for the advance payment and repayments in accordance with Sub-Clause 14.2 [*Advance Payment*];

(e)   any amounts to be added and deducted for Plant and Materials in accordance with Sub-Clause 14.5 [*Plant and Materials intended for the Works*];

(f)   any other additions or deductions which may have become due under the Contract or otherwise, including those under Clause 20 [*Claims, Disputes and Arbitration*]; and

(g)   the deduction of amounts certified in all previous Payment Certificates.

14.4

Schedule of Payments

If the Contract includes a schedule of payments specifying the instalments in which the Contract Price will be paid, then unless otherwise stated in this schedule:

(a)   the instalments quoted in this schedule of payments shall be the estimated contract values for the purposes of sub-paragraph (a) of Sub-Clause 14.3 [*Application for Interim Payment Certificates*];

(b)   Sub-Clause 14.5 [*Plant and Materials intended for the Works*] shall not apply; and

(c)   if these instalments are not defined by reference to the actual progress achieved in executing the Works, and if actual progress is found to be less than that on which this schedule of payments was based, then the Engineer may proceed in accordance with Sub-Clause 3.5 [*Determinations*] to agree or determine revised instalments, which shall take account of the extent to which progress is less than that on which the instalments were previously based.

If the Contract does not include a schedule of payments, the Contractor shall submit non-binding estimates of the payments which he expects to become due during each quarterly period. The first estimate shall be submitted within 42 days after the Commencement Date. Revised estimates shall be submitted at quarterly intervals, until the Taking-Over Certificate has been issued for the Works.

14.5

Plant and Materials intended for the Works

If this Sub-Clause applies, Interim Payment Certificates shall include, under sub-paragraph (e) of Sub-Clause 14.3, (i) an amount for Plant and Materials which have been sent to the Site for incorporation in the Permanent Works, and (ii) a reduction when the contract value of such Plant and Materials is included as part of the Permanent Works under sub-paragraph (a) of Sub-Clause 14.3 [*Application for Interim Payment Certificates*].

If the lists referred to in sub-paragraphs (b)(i) or (c)(i) below are not included in the Appendix to Tender, this Sub-Clause shall not apply.

The Engineer shall determine and certify each addition if the following conditions are satisfied:

(a)   the Contractor has:

(i)   kept satisfactory records (including the orders, receipts, Costs and use of Plant and Materials) which are available for inspection, and

(ii)   submitted a statement of the Cost of acquiring and delivering the Plant and Materials to the Site, supported by satisfactory evidence;

and either:

(b)   the relevant Plant and Materials:

(i)   are those listed in the Appendix to Tender for payment when shipped,

(ii)   have been shipped to the Country, en route to the Site, in accordance with the Contract; and

(iii)   are described in a clean shipped bill of lading or other evidence of shipment, which has been submitted to the Engineer together with evidence of payment of freight and insurance, any other documents reasonably required, and a bank guarantee in a form and issued by an entity approved by the Employer in amounts and currencies equal to the amount due under this Sub-Clause: this guarantee may be in a similar form to the form referred to in Sub-Clause 14.2 [*Advance Payment*] and shall be valid until the Plant and Materials are properly stored on Site and protected against loss, damage or deterioration;

or

(c)   the relevant Plant and Materials:

(i)   are those listed in the Appendix to Tender for payment when delivered to the Site, and

(ii)   have been delivered to and are properly stored on the Site, are protected against loss, damage or deterioration, and appear to be in accordance with the Contract.

The additional amount to be certified shall be the equivalent of eighty percent of the Engineer's determination of the cost of the Plant and Materials (including delivery to Site), taking account of the documents mentioned in this Sub-Clause and of the contract value of the Plant and Materials.

The currencies for this additional amount shall be the same as those in which payment will become due when the contract value is included under sub-paragraph (a) of Sub-Clause 14.3 [*Application for Interim Payment Certificates*]. At that time, the Payment Certificate shall include the applicable reduction which shall be equivalent to, and in the same currencies and proportions as, this additional amount for the relevant Plant and Materials.

14.6

Issue of Interim Payment Certificates

No amount will be certified or paid until the Employer has received and approved the Performance Security. Thereafter, the Engineer shall, within 28 days after receiving a Statement and supporting documents, issue to the Employer an Interim Payment Certificate which shall state the amount which the Engineer fairly determines to be due, with supporting particulars.

However, prior to issuing the Taking-Over Certificate for the Works, the Engineer shall not be bound to issue an Interim Payment Certificate in an amount which would (after retention and other deductions) be less than the minimum amount of Interim Payment Certificates (if any) stated in the Appendix to Tender. In this event, the Engineer shall give notice to the Contractor accordingly.

An Interim Payment Certificate shall not be withheld for any other reason, although:

(a) if any thing supplied or work done by the Contractor is not in accordance with the Contract, the cost of rectification or replacement may be withheld until rectification or replacement has been completed; and/or

(b) if the Contractor was or is failing to perform any work or obligation in accordance with the Contract, and had been so notified by the Engineer, the value of this work or obligation may be withheld until the work or obligation has been performed.

The Engineer may in any Payment Certificate make any correction or modification that should properly be made to any previous Payment Certificate. A Payment Certificate shall not be deemed to indicate the Engineer's acceptance, approval, consent or satisfaction.

14.7
Payment

The Employer shall pay to the Contractor:

(a) the first instalment of the advance payment within 42 days after issuing the Letter of Acceptance or within 21 days after receiving the documents in accordance with Sub-Clause 4.2 [*Performance Security*] and Sub-Clause 14.2 [*Advance Payment*], whichever is later;

(b) the amount certified in each Interim Payment Certificate within 56 days after the Engineer receives the Statement and supporting documents; and

(c) the amount certified in the Final Payment Certificate within 56 days after the Employer receives this Payment Certificate.

Payment of the amount due in each currency shall be made into the bank account, nominated by the Contractor, in the payment country (for this currency) specified in the Contract.

14.8
Delayed Payment

If the Contractor does not receive payment in accordance with Sub-Clause 14.7 [*Payment*], the Contractor shall be entitled to receive financing charges compounded monthly on the amount unpaid during the period of delay. This period shall be deemed to commence on the date for payment specified in Sub-Clause 14.7 [*Payment*], irrespective (in the case of its sub-paragraph (b)) of the date on which any Interim Payment Certificate is issued.

Unless otherwise stated in the Particular Conditions, these financing charges shall be calculated at the annual rate of three percentage points above the discount rate of the central bank in the country of the currency of payment, and shall be paid in such currency.

The Contractor shall be entitled to this payment without formal notice or certification, and without prejudice to any other right or remedy.

14.9
Payment of Retention Money

When the Taking-Over Certificate has been issued for the Works, the first half of the Retention Money shall be certified by the Engineer for payment to the Contractor. If a Taking-Over Certificate is issued for a Section or part of the Works, a proportion of the Retention Money shall be certified and paid. This proportion shall be two-fifths (40%) of the proportion calculated by dividing the estimated contract value of the Section or part, by the estimated final Contract Price.

Promptly after the latest of the expiry dates of the Defects Notification Periods, the outstanding balance of the Retention Money shall be certified by the Engineer for payment to the Contractor. If a Taking-Over Certificate was issued for a Section, a proportion of the second half of the Retention Money shall be certified and paid promptly after the expiry date of the Defects Notification Period for the Section. This proportion shall be two-fifths (40%) of the proportion calculated by dividing the estimated contract value of the Section by the estimated final Contract Price.

However, if any work remains to be executed under Clause 11 [*Defects Liability*], the Engineer shall be entitled to withhold certification of the estimated cost of this work until it has been executed.

When calculating these proportions, no account shall be taken of any adjustments under Sub-Clause 13.7 [*Adjustments for Changes in Legislation*] and Sub-Clause 13.8 [*Adjustments for Changes in Cost*].

14.10

Statement at Completion

Within 84 days after receiving the Taking-Over Certificate for the Works, the Contractor shall submit to the Engineer six copies of a Statement at completion with supporting documents, in accordance with Sub-Clause 14.3 [*Application for Interim Payment Certificates*], showing:

(a) the value of all work done in accordance with the Contract up to the date stated in the Taking-Over Certificate for the Works,
(b) any further sums which the Contractor considers to be due, and
(c) an estimate of any other amounts which the Contractor considers will become due to him under the Contract. Estimated amounts shall be shown separately in this Statement at completion.

The Engineer shall then certify in accordance with Sub-Clause 14.6 [*Issue of Interim Payment Certificates*].

14.11

Application for Final Payment Certificate

Within 56 days after receiving the Performance Certificate, the Contractor shall submit, to the Engineer, six copies of a draft final statement with supporting documents showing in detail in a form approved by the Engineer:

(a) the value of all work done in accordance with the Contract, and
(b) any further sums which the Contractor considers to be due to him under the Contract or otherwise.

If the Engineer disagrees with or cannot verify any part of the draft final statement, the Contractor shall submit such further information as the Engineer may reasonably require and shall make such changes in the draft as may be agreed between them. The Contractor shall then prepare and submit to the Engineer the final statement as agreed. This agreed statement is referred to in these Conditions as the "Final Statement".

However if, following discussions between the Engineer and the Contractor and any changes to the draft final statement which are agreed, it becomes evident that a dispute exists, the Engineer shall deliver to the Employer (with a copy to the Contractor) an Interim Payment Certificate for the agreed parts of the draft final statement. Thereafter, if the dispute is finally resolved under Sub-Clause 20.4 [*Obtaining Dispute Adjudication Board's Decision*] or Sub-Clause 20.5 [*Amicable Settlement*], the Contractor shall then prepare and submit to the Employer (with a copy to the Engineer) a Final Statement.

14.12

Discharge

When submitting the Final Statement, the Contractor shall submit a written discharge which confirms that the total of the Final Statement represents full and final settlement of all moneys due to the Contractor under or in connection with the Contract. This discharge may state that it becomes effective when the Contractor has received the Performance Security and the outstanding balance of this total, in which event the discharge shall be effective on such date.

14.13

Issue of Final Payment Certificate

Within 28 days after receiving the Final Statement and written discharge in accordance with Sub-Clause 14.11 [*Application for Final Payment Certificate*] and Sub-Clause 14.12 [*Discharge*], the Engineer shall issue, to the Employer, the Final Payment Certificate which shall state:

(a)   the amount which is finally due, and

(b)   after giving credit to the Employer for all amounts previously paid by the Employer and for all sums to which the Employer is entitled, the balance (if any) due from the Employer to the Contractor or from the Contractor to the Employer, as the case may be.

If the Contractor has not applied for a Final Payment Certificate in accordance with Sub-Clause 14.11 [*Application for Final Payment Certificate*] and Sub-Clause 14.12 [*Discharge*], the Engineer shall request the Contractor to do so. If the Contractor fails to submit an application within a period of 28 days, the Engineer shall issue the Final Payment Certificate for such amount as he fairly determines to be due.

14.14

Cessation of Employer's Liability

The Employer shall not be liable to the Contractor for any matter or thing under or in connection with the Contract or execution of the Works, except to the extent that the Contractor shall have included an amount expressly for it:

(a)   in the Final Statement and also

(b)   (except for matters or things arising after the issue of the Taking-Over Certificate for the Works) in the Statement at completion described in Sub-Clause 14.10 [*Statement at Completion*].

However, this Sub-Clause shall not limit the Employer's liability under his indemn-ification obligations, or the Employer's liability in any case of fraud, deliberate default or reckless misconduct by the Employer.

14.15

Currencies of Payment

The Contract Price shall be paid in the currency or currencies named in the Appendix to Tender. Unless otherwise stated in the Particular Conditions, if more than one currency is so named, payments shall be made as follows:

(a)   if the Accepted Contract Amount was expressed in Local Currency only:

(i)   the proportions or amounts of the Local and Foreign Currencies, and the fixed rates of exchange to be used for calculating the payments, shall be as stated in the Appendix to Tender, except as otherwise agreed by both Parties;

(ii)   payments and deductions under Sub-Clause 13.5 [*Provisional Sums*] and Sub-Clause 13.7 [*Adjustments for Changes in Legislation*] shall be made in the applicable currencies and proportions; and

(iii) other payments and deductions under sub-paragraphs (a) to (d) of Sub-Clause 14.3 [*Application for Interim Payment Certificates*] shall be made in the currencies and proportions specified in sub-paragraph (a)(i) above;

(b)   payment of the damages specified in the Appendix to Tender shall be made in the currencies and proportions specified in the Appendix to Tender;

(c)   other payments to the Employer by the Contractor shall be made in the currency in which the sum was expended by the Employer, or in such currency as may be agreed by both Parties;

(d)   if any amount payable by the Contractor to the Employer in a particular currency exceeds the sum payable by the Employer to the Contractor in that currency, the Employer may recover the balance of this amount from the sums otherwise payable to the Contractor in other currencies; and

(e)   if no rates of exchange are stated in the Appendix to Tender, they shall be those prevailing on the Base Date and determined by the central bank of the Country.

15 Termination by Employer

15.1
Notice to Correct

If the Contractor fails to carry out any obligation under the Contract, the Engineer may by notice require the Contractor to make good the failure and to remedy it within a specified reasonable time.

15.2
Termination by Employer

The Employer shall be entitled to terminate the Contract if the Contractor:

(a)   fails to comply with Sub-Clause 4.2 [*Performance Security*] or with a notice under Sub-Clause 15.1 [*Notice to Correct*],

(b)   abandons the Works or otherwise plainly demonstrates the intention not to continue performance of his obligations under the Contract,

(c)   without reasonable excuse fails:

    (i)   to proceed with the Works in accordance with Clause 8 [*Commencement, Delays and Suspension*], or

    (ii)   to comply with a notice issued under Sub-Clause 7.5 [*Rejection*] or Sub-Clause 7.6 [*Remedial Work*], within 28 days after receiving it,

(d)   subcontracts the whole of the Works or assigns the Contract without the required agreement,

(e)   becomes bankrupt or insolvent, goes into liquidation, has a receiving or administration order made against him, compounds with his creditors, or carries on business under a receiver, trustee or manager for the benefit of his creditors, or if any act is done or event occurs which (under applicable Laws) has a similar effect to any of these acts or events, or

(f)   gives or offers to give (directly or indirectly) to any person any bribe, gift, gratuity, commission or other thing of value, as an inducement or reward:

    (i)   for doing or forbearing to do any action in relation to the Contract, or

    (ii)   for showing or forbearing to show favour or disfavour to any person in relation to the Contract,

or if any of the Contractor's Personnel, agents or Subcontractors gives or offers to give (directly or indirectly) to any person any such inducement or reward as is described in this sub-paragraph (f). However, lawful inducements and rewards to Contractor's Personnel shall not entitle termination.

In any of these events or circumstances, the Employer may, upon giving 14 days' notice to the Contractor, terminate the Contract and expel the Contractor from the Site. However, in the case of sub-paragraph (e) or (f), the Employer may by notice terminate the Contract immediately.

The Employer's election to terminate the Contract shall not prejudice any other rights of the Employer, under the Contract or otherwise.

The Contractor shall then leave the Site and deliver any required Goods, all Contractor's Documents, and other design documents made by or for him, to the Engineer. However, the Contractor shall use his best efforts to comply immediately with any reasonable instructions included in the notice (i) for the assignment of any subcontract, and (ii) for the protection of life or property or for the safety of the Works.

After termination, the Employer may complete the Works and/or arrange for any other entities to do so. The Employer and these entities may then use any Goods, Contractor's Documents and other design documents made by or on behalf of the Contractor.

The Employer shall then give notice that the Contractor's Equipment and Temporary Works will be released to the Contractor at or near the Site. The Contractor shall promptly arrange their removal, at the risk and cost of the Contractor. However, if by this time the Contractor has failed to make a payment due to the Employer, these items may be sold by the Employer in order to recover this payment. Any balance of the proceeds shall then be paid to the Contractor.

15.3

Valuation at Date of Termination

As soon as practicable after a notice of termination under Sub-Clause 15.2 [*Termination by Employer*] has taken effect, the Engineer shall proceed in accordance with Sub-Clause 3.5 [*Determinations*] to agree or determine the value of the Works, Goods and Contractor's Documents, and any other sums due to the Contractor for work executed in accordance with the Contract.

15.4

Payment after Termination

After a notice of termination under Sub-Clause 15.2 [*Termination by Employer*] has taken effect, the Employer may:

(a)   proceed in accordance with Sub-Clause 2.5 [*Employer's Claims*],

(b)   withhold further payments to the Contractor until the costs of execution, completion and remedying of any defects, damages for delay in completion (if any), and all other costs incurred by the Employer, have been established, and/or

(c)   recover from the Contractor any losses and damages incurred by the Employer and any extra costs of completing the Works, after allowing for any sum due to the Contractor under Sub-Clause 15.3 [*Valuation at Date of Termination*]. After recovering any such losses, damages and extra costs, the Employer shall pay any balance to the Contractor.

15.5

Employer's Entitlement to Termination

The Employer shall be entitled to terminate the Contract, at any time for the Employer's convenience, by giving notice of such termination to the Contractor. The termination shall take effect 28 days after the later of the dates on which the Contractor receives this notice or the Employer returns the Performance Security. The Employer shall not terminate the Contract under this Sub-Clause in order to execute the Works himself or to arrange for the Works to be executed by another contractor.

After this termination, the Contractor shall proceed in accordance with Sub-Clause 16.3 [*Cessation of Work and Removal of Contractor's Equipment*] and shall be paid in accordance with Sub-Clause 19.6 [*Optional Termination, Payment and Release*].

16 Suspension and Termination by Contractor

16.1
Contractor's Entitlement to Suspend Work

If the Engineer fails to certify in accordance with Sub-Clause 14.6 [*Issue of Interim Payment Certificates*] or the Employer fails to comply with Sub-Clause 2.4 [*Employer's Financial Arrangements*] or Sub-Clause 14.7 [*Payment*], the Contractor may, after giving not less than 21 days' notice to the Employer, suspend work (or reduce the rate of work) unless and until the Contractor has received the Payment Certificate, reasonable evidence or payment, as the case may be and as described in the notice.

The Contractor's action shall not prejudice his entitlements to financing charges under Sub-Clause 14.8 [*Delayed Payment*] and to termination under Sub-Clause 16.2 [*Termination by Contractor*].

If the Contractor subsequently receives such Payment Certificate, evidence or payment (as described in the relevant Sub-Clause and in the above notice) before giving a notice of termination, the Contractor shall resume normal working as soon as is reasonably practicable.

If the Contractor suffers delay and/or incurs Cost as a result of suspending work (or reducing the rate of work) in accordance with this Sub-Clause, the Contractor shall give notice to the Engineer and shall be entitled subject to Sub-Clause 20.1 [*Contractor's Claims*] to:

(a) an extension of time for any such delay, if completion is or will be delayed, under Sub-Clause 8.4 [*Extension of Time for Completion*], and

(b) payment of any such Cost plus reasonable profit, which shall be included in the Contract Price.

After receiving this notice, the Engineer shall proceed in accordance with Sub-Clause 3.5 [*Determinations*] to agree or determine these matters.

16.2
Termination by Contractor

The Contractor shall be entitled to terminate the Contract if:

(a) the Contractor does not receive the reasonable evidence within 42 days after giving notice under Sub-Clause 16.1 [*Contractor's Entitlement to Suspend Work*] in respect of a failure to comply with Sub-Clause 2.4 [*Employer's Financial Arrangements*],

(b) the Engineer fails, within 56 days after receiving a Statement and supporting documents, to issue the relevant Payment Certificate,

(c) the Contractor does not receive the amount due under an Interim Payment Certificate within 42 days after the expiry of the time stated in Sub-Clause 14.7 [*Payment*] within which payment is to be made (except for deductions in accordance with Sub-Clause 2.5 [*Employer's Claims*]),

(d) the Employer substantially fails to perform his obligations under the Contract,

(e) the Employer fails to comply with Sub-Clause 1.6 [*Contract Agreement*] or Sub-Clause 1.7 [*Assignment*],

(f) a prolonged suspension affects the whole of the Works as described in Sub-Clause 8.11 [*Prolonged Suspension*], or

(g) the Employer becomes bankrupt or insolvent, goes into liquidation, has a receiving or administration order made against him, compounds with his creditors, or carries on business under a receiver, trustee or manager for the benefit of his creditors, or if any act is done or event occurs which (under applicable Laws) has a similar effect to any of these acts or events.

In any of these events or circumstances, the Contractor may, upon giving 14 days' notice to the Employer, terminate the Contract. However, in the case of sub-paragraph (f) or (g), the Contractor may by notice terminate the Contract immediately.

The Contractor's election to terminate the Contract shall not prejudice any other rights of the Contractor, under the Contract or otherwise.

Cessation of Work and Removal of Contractor's Equipment

After a notice of termination under Sub-Clause 15.5 [*Employer's Entitlement to Termination*], Sub-Clause 16.2 [*Termination by Contractor*] or Sub-Clause 19.6 [*Optional Termination, Payment and Release*] has taken effect, the Contractor shall promptly:

(a) cease all further work, except for such work as may have been instructed by the Engineer for the protection of life or property or for the safety of the Works,

(b) hand over Contractor's Documents, Plant, Materials and other work, for which the Contractor has received payment, and

(c) remove all other Goods from the Site, except as necessary for safety, and leave the Site.

Payment on Termination

After a notice of termination under Sub-Clause 16.2 [*Termination by Contractor*] has taken effect, the Employer shall promptly:

(a) return the Performance Security to the Contractor,

(b) pay the Contractor in accordance with Sub-Clause 19.6 [*Optional Termination, Payment and Release*], and

(c) pay to the Contractor the amount of any loss of profit or other loss or damage sustained by the Contractor as a result of this termination.

17 Risk and Responsibility

17.1

Indemnities

The Contractor shall indemnify and hold harmless the Employer, the Employer's Personnel, and their respective agents, against and from all claims, damages, losses and expenses (including legal fees and expenses) in respect of:

(a) bodily injury, sickness, disease or death, of any person whatsoever arising out of or in the course of or by reason of the Contractor's design (if any), the execution and completion of the Works and the remedying of any defects, unless attributable to any negligence, wilful act or breach of the Contract by the Employer, the Employer's Personnel, or any of their respective agents, and

(b) damage to or loss of any property, real or personal (other than the Works), to the extent that such damage or loss:

(i) arises out of or in the course of or by reason of the Contractor's design (if any), the execution and completion of the Works and the remedying of any defects, and

(ii) is attributable to any negligence, wilful act or breach of the Contract by the Contractor, the Contractor's Personnel, their respective agents, or anyone directly or indirectly employed by any of them.

© FIDIC 1999
Conditions of Contract for Construction

The Employer shall indemnify and hold harmless the Contractor, the Contractor's Personnel, and their respective agents, against and from all claims, damages, losses and expenses (including legal fees and expenses) in respect of (1) bodily injury, sickness, disease or death, which is attributable to any negligence, wilful act or breach of the Contract by the Employer, the Employer's Personnel, or any of their respective agents, and (2) the matters for which liability may be excluded from insurance cover, as described in sub-paragraphs (d)(i), (ii) and (iii) of Sub-Clause 18.3 [*Insurance Against Injury to Persons and Damage to Property*].

17.2
Contractor's Care of the Works

The Contractor shall take full responsibility for the care of the Works and Goods from the Commencement Date until the Taking-Over Certificate is issued (or is deemed to be issued under Sub-Clause 10.1 [*Taking Over of the Works and Sections*]) for the Works, when responsibility for the care of the Works shall pass to the Employer. If a Taking-Over Certificate is issued (or is so deemed to be issued) for any Section or part of the Works, responsibility for the care of the Section or part shall then pass to the Employer.

After responsibility has accordingly passed to the Employer, the Contractor shall take responsibility for the care of any work which is outstanding on the date stated in a Taking-Over Certificate, until this outstanding work has been completed.

If any loss or damage happens to the Works, Goods or Contractor's Documents during the period when the Contractor is responsible for their care, from any cause not listed in Sub-Clause 17.3 [*Employer's Risks*], the Contractor shall rectify the loss or damage at the Contractor's risk and cost, so that the Works, Goods and Contractor's Documents conform with the Contract.

The Contractor shall be liable for any loss or damage caused by any actions performed by the Contractor after a Taking-Over Certificate has been issued. The Contractor shall also be liable for any loss or damage which occurs after a Taking-Over Certificate has been issued and which arose from a previous event for which the Contractor was liable.

17.3
Employer's Risks

The risks referred to in Sub-Clause 17.4 below are:

(a) war, hostilities (whether war be declared or not), invasion, act of foreign enemies,

(b) rebellion, terrorism, revolution, insurrection, military or usurped power, or civil war, within the Country,

(c) riot, commotion or disorder within the Country by persons other than the Contractor's Personnel and other employees of the Contractor and Subcontractors,

(d) munitions of war, explosive materials, ionising radiation or contamination by radio-activity, within the Country, except as may be attributable to the Contractor's use of such munitions, explosives, radiation or radio-activity,

(e) pressure waves caused by aircraft or other aerial devices travelling at sonic or supersonic speeds,

(f) use or occupation by the Employer of any part of the Permanent Works, except as may be specified in the Contract,

(g) design of any part of the Works by the Employer's Personnel or by others for whom the Employer is responsible, and

(h) any operation of the forces of nature which is Unforeseeable or against which an experienced contractor could not reasonably have been expected to have taken adequate preventative precautions.

17.4

Consequences of Employer's Risks

If and to the extent that any of the risks listed in Sub-Clause 17.3 above results in loss or damage to the Works, Goods or Contractor's Documents, the Contractor shall promptly give notice to the Engineer and shall rectify this loss or damage to the extent required by the Engineer.

If the Contractor suffers delay and/or incurs Cost from rectifying this loss or damage, the Contractor shall give a further notice to the Engineer and shall be entitled subject to Sub-Clause 20.1 [*Contractor's Claims*] to:

(a) an extension of time for any such delay, if completion is or will be delayed, under Sub-Clause 8.4 [*Extension of Time for Completion*], and

(b) payment of any such Cost, which shall be included in the Contract Price. In the case of sub-paragraphs (f) and (g) of Sub-Clause 17.3 [*Employer's Risks*], reasonable profit on the Cost shall also be included.

After receiving this further notice, the Engineer shall proceed in accordance with Sub-Clause 3.5 [*Determinations*] to agree or determine these matters.

17.5

Intellectual and Industrial Property Rights

In this Sub-Clause, "infringement" means an infringement (or alleged infringement) of any patent, registered design, copyright, trade mark, trade name, trade secret or other intellectual or industrial property right relating to the Works; and "claim" means a claim (or proceedings pursuing a claim) alleging an infringement.

Whenever a Party does not give notice to the other Party of any claim within 28 days of receiving the claim, the first Party shall be deemed to have waived any right to indemnity under this Sub-Clause.

The Employer shall indemnify and hold the Contractor harmless against and from any claim alleging an infringement which is or was:

(a) an unavoidable result of the Contractor's compliance with the Contract, or

(b) a result of any Works being used by the Employer:

(i) for a purpose other than that indicated by, or reasonably to be inferred from, the Contract, or

(ii) in conjunction with any thing not supplied by the Contractor, unless such use was disclosed to the Contractor prior to the Base Date or is stated in the Contract.

The Contractor shall indemnify and hold the Employer harmless against and from any other claim which arises out of or in relation to (i) the manufacture, use, sale or import of any Goods, or (ii) any design for which the Contractor is responsible.

If a Party is entitled to be indemnified under this Sub-Clause, the indemnifying Party may (at its cost) conduct negotiations for the settlement of the claim, and any litigation or arbitration which may arise from it. The other Party shall, at the request and cost of the indemnifying Party, assist in contesting the claim. This other Party (and its Personnel) shall not make any admission which might be prejudicial to the indemnifying Party, unless the indemnifying Party failed to take over the conduct of any negotiations, litigation or arbitration upon being requested to do so by such other Party.

17.6

Limitation of Liability

Neither Party shall be liable to the other Party for loss of use of any Works, loss of profit, loss of any contract or for any indirect or consequential loss or damage which may be suffered by the other Party in connection with the Contract, other than under

Sub-Clause 16.4 [*Payment on Termination*] and Sub-Clause 17.1 [*Indemnities*].

The total liability of the Contractor to the Employer, under or in connection with the Contract other than under Sub-Clause 4.19 [*Electricity, Water and Gas*], Sub-Clause 4.20 [*Employer's Equipment and Free-Issue Material*], Sub-Clause 17.1 [*Indemnities*] and Sub-Clause 17.5 [*Intellectual and Industrial Property Rights*], shall not exceed the sum stated in the Particular Conditions or (if a sum is not so stated) the Accepted Contract Amount.

This Sub-Clause shall not limit liability in any case of fraud, deliberate default or reckless misconduct by the defaulting Party.

18 Insurance

18.1
General Requirements for Insurances

In this Clause, "insuring Party" means, for each type of insurance, the Party responsible for effecting and maintaining the insurance specified in the relevant Sub-Clause.

Wherever the Contractor is the insuring Party, each insurance shall be effected with insurers and in terms approved by the Employer. These terms shall be consistent with any terms agreed by both Parties before the date of the Letter of Acceptance. This agreement of terms shall take precedence over the provisions of this Clause.

Wherever the Employer is the insuring Party, each insurance shall be effected with insurers and in terms consistent with the details annexed to the Particular Conditions.

If a policy is required to indemnify joint insured, the cover shall apply separately to each insured as though a separate policy had been issued for each of the joint insured. If a policy indemnifies additional joint insured, namely in addition to the insured specified in this Clause, (i) the Contractor shall act under the policy on behalf of these additional joint insured except that the Employer shall act for Employer's Personnel, (ii) additional joint insured shall not be entitled to receive payments directly from the insurer or to have any other direct dealings with the insurer, and (iii) the insuring Party shall require all additional joint insured to comply with the conditions stipulated in the policy.

Each policy insuring against loss or damage shall provide for payments to be made in the currencies required to rectify the loss or damage. Payments received from insurers shall be used for the rectification of the loss or damage.

The relevant insuring Party shall, within the respective periods stated in the Appendix to Tender (calculated from the Commencement Date), submit to the other Party:

(a)   evidence that the insurances described in this Clause have been effected, and
(b)   copies of the policies for the insurances described in Sub-Clause 18.2 [*Insurance for Works and Contractor's Equipment*] and Sub-Clause 18.3 [*Insurance against Injury to Persons and Damage to Property*].

When each premium is paid, the insuring Party shall submit evidence of payment to the other Party. Whenever evidence or policies are submitted, the insuring Party shall also give notice to the Engineer.

Each Party shall comply with the conditions stipulated in each of the insurance policies. The insuring Party shall keep the insurers informed of any relevant changes to the execution of the Works and ensure that insurance is maintained in accordance with this Clause.

Neither Party shall make any material alteration to the terms of any insurance without the prior approval of the other Party. If an insurer makes (or attempts to make) any alteration, the Party first notified by the insurer shall promptly give notice to the other Party.

If the insuring Party fails to effect and keep in force any of the insurances it is required to effect and maintain under the Contract, or fails to provide satisfactory evidence and copies of policies in accordance with this Sub-Clause, the other Party may (at its option and without prejudice to any other right or remedy) effect insurance for the relevant coverage and pay the premiums due. The insuring Party shall pay the amount of these premiums to the other Party, and the Contract Price shall be adjusted accordingly.

Nothing in this Clause limits the obligations, liabilities or responsibilities of the Contractor or the Employer, under the other terms of the Contract or otherwise. Any amounts not insured or not recovered from the insurers shall be borne by the Contractor and/or the Employer in accordance with these obligations, liabilities or responsibilities. However, if the insuring Party fails to effect and keep in force an insurance which is available and which it is required to effect and maintain under the Contract, and the other Party neither approves the omission nor effects insurance for the coverage relevant to this default, any moneys which should have been recoverable under this insurance shall be paid by the insuring Party.

Payments by one Party to the other Party shall be subject to Sub-Clause 2.5 [*Employer's Claims*] or Sub-Clause 20.1 [*Contractor's Claims*], as applicable.

18.2

Insurance for Works and Contractor's Equipment

The insuring Party shall insure the Works, Plant, Materials and Contractor's Documents for not less than the full reinstatement cost including the costs of demolition, removal of debris and professional fees and profit. This insurance shall be effective from the date by which the evidence is to be submitted under sub-paragraph (a) of Sub-Clause 18.1 [*General Requirements for Insurances*], until the date of issue of the Taking-Over Certificate for the Works.

The insuring Party shall maintain this insurance to provide cover until the date of issue of the Performance Certificate, for loss or damage for which the Contractor is liable arising from a cause occurring prior to the issue of the Taking-Over Certificate, and for loss or damage caused by the Contractor in the course of any other operations (including those under Clause 11 [*Defects Liability*]).

The insuring Party shall insure the Contractor's Equipment for not less than the full replacement value, including delivery to Site. For each item of Contractor's Equipment, the insurance shall be effective while it is being transported to the Site and until it is no longer required as Contractor's Equipment.

Unless otherwise stated in the Particular Conditions, insurances under this Sub-Clause:

(a)   shall be effected and maintained by the Contractor as insuring Party,

(b)   shall be in the joint names of the Parties, who shall be jointly entitled to receive payments from the insurers, payments being held or allocated between the Parties for the sole purpose of rectifying the loss or damage,

(c)   shall cover all loss and damage from any cause not listed in Sub-Clause 17.3 [*Employer's Risks*],

(d)   shall also cover loss or damage to a part of the Works which is attributable to the use or occupation by the Employer of another part of the Works, and loss or damage from the risks listed in sub-paragraphs (c), (g) and (h) of Sub-Clause 17.3 [*Employer's Risks*], excluding (in each case) risks which are not insurable at commercially reasonable terms, with deductibles per occurrence of not more than the amount stated in the Appendix to Tender (if an amount is not so stated, this sub-paragraph (d) shall not apply), and

(e)   may however exclude loss of, damage to, and reinstatement of:

(i)   a part of the Works which is in a defective condition due to a defect in its design, materials or workmanship (but cover shall include any other parts which are lost or damaged as a direct result of this defective condition and not as described in sub-paragraph (ii) below),

(ii)   a part of the Works which is lost or damaged in order to reinstate any other part of the Works if this other part is in a defective condition due to a defect in its design, materials or workmanship,

(iii)   a part of the Works which has been taken over by the Employer, except to the extent that the Contractor is liable for the loss or damage, and

(iv)   Goods while they are not in the Country, subject to Sub-Clause 14.5 [*Plant and Materials intended for the Works*].

If, more than one year after the Base Date, the cover described in sub-paragraph (d) above ceases to be available at commercially reasonable terms, the Contractor shall (as insuring Party) give notice to the Employer, with supporting particulars. The Employer shall then (i) be entitled subject to Sub-Clause 2.5 [*Employer's Claims*] to payment of an amount equivalent to such commercially reasonable terms as the Contractor should have expected to have paid for such cover, and (ii) be deemed, unless he obtains the cover at commercially reasonable terms, to have approved the omission under Sub-Clause 18.1 [*General Requirements for Insurances*].

18.3

Insurance against Injury to Persons and Damage to Property

The insuring Party shall insure against each Party's liability for any loss, damage, death or bodily injury which may occur to any physical property (except things insured under Sub-Clause 18.2 [*Insurance for Works and Contractor's Equipment*]) or to any person (except persons insured under Sub-Clause 18.4 [*Insurance for Contractor's Personnel*]), which may arise out of the Contractor's performance of the Contract and occurring before the issue of the Performance Certificate.

This insurance shall be for a limit per occurrence of not less than the amount stated in the Appendix to Tender, with no limit on the number of occurrences. If an amount is not stated in the Appendix to Tender, this Sub-Clause shall not apply.

Unless otherwise stated in the Particular Conditions, the insurances specified in this Sub-Clause:

(a)   shall be effected and maintained by the Contractor as insuring Party,

(b)   shall be in the joint names of the Parties,

(c)   shall be extended to cover liability for all loss and damage to the Employer's property (except things insured under Sub-Clause 18.2) arising out of the Contractor's performance of the Contract, and

(d)   may however exclude liability to the extent that it arises from:

(i)   the Employer's right to have the Permanent Works executed on, over, under, in or through any land, and to occupy this land for the Permanent Works,

(ii)   damage which is an unavoidable result of the Contractor's obligations to execute the Works and remedy any defects, and

(iii)   a cause listed in Sub-Clause 17.3 [*Employer's Risks*], except to the extent that cover is available at commercially reasonable terms.

18.4

Insurance for Contractor's Personnel

The Contractor shall effect and maintain insurance against liability for claims, damages, losses and expenses (including legal fees and expenses) arising from injury, sickness, disease or death of any person employed by the Contractor or any other of the Contractor's Personnel.

The Employer and the Engineer shall also be indemnified under the policy of insurance, except that this insurance may exclude losses and claims to the extent that they arise from any act or neglect of the Employer or of the Employer's Personnel.

The insurance shall be maintained in full force and effect during the whole time that these personnel are assisting in the execution of the Works. For a Subcontractor's employees, the insurance may be effected by the Subcontractor, but the Contractor shall be responsible for compliance with this Clause.

Force Majeure

19.1
Definition of Force Majeure

In this Clause, "Force Majeure" means an exceptional event or circumstance:

(a)   which is beyond a Party's control,

(b)   which such Party could not reasonably have provided against before entering into the Contract,

(c)   which, having arisen, such Party could not reasonably have avoided or overcome, and

(d)   which is not substantially attributable to the other Party.

Force Majeure may include, but is not limited to, exceptional events or circumstances of the kind listed below, so long as conditions (a) to (d) above are satisfied:

(i)   war, hostilities (whether war be declared or not), invasion, act of foreign enemies,

(ii)   rebellion, terrorism, revolution, insurrection, military or usurped power, or civil war,

(iii)   riot, commotion, disorder, strike or lockout by persons other than the Contractor's Personnel and other employees of the Contractor and Sub-contractors,

(iv)   munitions of war, explosive materials, ionising radiation or contamination by radio-activity, except as may be attributable to the Contractor's use of such munitions, explosives, radiation or radio-activity, and

(v)   natural catastrophes such as earthquake, hurricane, typhoon or volcanic activity.

19.2

Notice of Force Majeure

If a Party is or will be prevented from performing any of its obligations under the Contract by Force Majeure, then it shall give notice to the other Party of the event or circumstances constituting the Force Majeure and shall specify the obligations, the performance of which is or will be prevented. The notice shall be given within 14 days after the Party became aware, or should have become aware, of the relevant event or circumstance constituting Force Majeure.

Conditions of Contract for Construction

The Party shall, having given notice, be excused performance of such obligations for so long as such Force Majeure prevents it from performing them.

Notwithstanding any other provision of this Clause, Force Majeure shall not apply to obligations of either Party to make payments to the other Party under the Contract.

19.3

Duty to Minimise Delay

Each Party shall at all times use all reasonable endeavours to minimise any delay in the performance of the Contract as a result of Force Majeure.

A Party shall give notice to the other Party when it ceases to be affected by the Force Majeure.

19.4

Consequences of Force Majeure

If the Contractor is prevented from performing any of his obligations under the Contract by Force Majeure of which notice has been given under Sub-Clause 19.2 [*Notice of Force Majeure*], and suffers delay and/or incurs Cost by reason of such Force Majeure, the Contractor shall be entitled subject to Sub-Clause 20.1 [*Contractor's Claims*] to:

(a)   an extension of time for any such delay, if completion is or will be delayed, under Sub-Clause 8.4 [*Extension of Time for Completion*], and

(b)   if the event or circumstance is of the kind described in sub-paragraphs (i) to (iv) of Sub-Clause 19.1 [*Definition of Force Majeure*] and, in the case of sub-paragraphs (ii) to (iv), occurs in the Country, payment of any such Cost.

After receiving this notice, the Engineer shall proceed in accordance with Sub-Clause 3.5 [*Determinations*] to agree or determine these matters.

19.5

Force Majeure Affecting Subcontractor

If any Subcontractor is entitled under any contract or agreement relating to the Works to relief from force majeure on terms additional to or broader than those specified in this Clause, such additional or broader force majeure events or circumstances shall not excuse the Contractor's non-performance or entitle him to relief under this Clause.

19.6

Optional Termination, Payment and Release

If the execution of substantially all the Works in progress is prevented for a continuous period of 84 days by reason of Force Majeure of which notice has been given under Sub-Clause 19.2 [*Notice of Force Majeure*], or for multiple periods which total more than 140 days due to the same notified Force Majeure, then either Party may give to the other Party a notice of termination of the Contract. In this event, the termination shall take effect 7 days after the notice is given, and the Contractor shall proceed in accordance with Sub-Clause 16.3 [*Cessation of Work and Removal of Contractor's Equipment*].

Upon such termination, the Engineer shall determine the value of the work done and issue a Payment Certificate which shall include:

(a)   the amounts payable for any work carried out for which a price is stated in the Contract;

(b)   the Cost of Plant and Materials ordered for the Works which have been delivered to the Contractor, or of which the Contractor is liable to accept delivery: this Plant and Materials shall become the property of (and be at the risk of) the Employer when paid for by the Employer, and the Contractor shall place the same at the Employer's disposal;

(c)   any other Cost or liability which in the circumstances was reasonably incurred by the Contractor in the expectation of completing the Works;

(d)   the Cost of removal of Temporary Works and Contractor's Equipment from the Site and the return of these items to the Contractor's works in his country (or to any other destination at no greater cost); and

(e)   the Cost of repatriation of the Contractor's staff and labour employed wholly in connection with the Works at the date of termination.

19.7

Release from Performance under the Law

Notwithstanding any other provision of this Clause, if any event or circumstance outside the control of the Parties (including, but not limited to, Force Majeure) arises which makes it impossible or unlawful for either or both Parties to fulfil its or their contractual obligations or which, under the law governing the Contract, entitles the Parties to be released from further performance of the Contract, then upon notice by either Party to the other Party of such event or circumstance:

(a)   the Parties shall be discharged from further performance, without prejudice to the rights of either Party in respect of any previous breach of the Contract, and

(b)   the sum payable by the Employer to the Contractor shall be the same as would have been payable under Sub-Clause 19.6 [*Optional Termination, Payment and Release*] if the Contract had been terminated under Sub-Clause 19.6.

20 Claim, Disputes and Arbitration

20.1

Contractor's Claims

If the Contractor considers himself to be entitled to any extension of the Time for Completion and/or any additional payment, under any Clause of these Conditions or otherwise in connection with the Contract, the Contractor shall give notice to the Engineer, describing the event or circumstance giving rise to the claim. The notice shall be given as soon as practicable, and not later than 28 days after the Contractor became aware, or should have become aware, of the event or circumstance.

If the Contractor fails to give notice of a claim within such period of 28 days, the Time for Completion shall not be extended, the Contractor shall not be entitled to additional payment, and the Employer shall be discharged from all liability in connection with the claim. Otherwise, the following provisions of this Sub-Clause shall apply.

The Contractor shall also submit any other notices which are required by the Contract, and supporting particulars for the claim, all as relevant to such event or circumstance.

The Contractor shall keep such contemporary records as may be necessary to substantiate any claim, either on the Site or at another location acceptable to the Engineer. Without admitting the Employer's liability, the Engineer may, after receiving any notice under this Sub-Clause, monitor the record-keeping and/or instruct the Contractor to keep further contemporary records. The Contractor shall permit the Engineer to inspect all these records, and shall (if instructed) submit copies to the Engineer.

Within 42 days after the Contractor became aware (or should have become aware) of the event or circumstance giving rise to the claim, or within such other period as may be proposed by the Contractor and approved by the Engineer, the Contractor shall send to the Engineer a fully detailed claim which includes full supporting particulars of the basis of the claim and of the extension of time and/or additional payment claimed. If the event or circumstance giving rise to the claim has a continuing effect:

(a)   this fully detailed claim shall be considered as interim;

Conditions of Contract for Construction

(b)   the Contractor shall send further interim claims at monthly intervals, giving the accumulated delay and/or amount claimed, and such further particulars as the Engineer may reasonably require; and

(c)   the Contractor shall send a final claim within 28 days after the end of the effects resulting from the event or circumstance, or within such other period as may be proposed by the Contractor and approved by the Engineer.

Within 42 days after receiving a claim or any further particulars supporting a previous claim, or within such other period as may be proposed by the Engineer and approved by the Contractor, the Engineer shall respond with approval, or with disapproval and detailed comments. He may also request any necessary further particulars, but shall nevertheless give his response on the principles of the claim within such time.

Each Payment Certificate shall include such amounts for any claim as have been reasonably substantiated as due under the relevant provision of the Contract. Unless and until the particulars supplied are sufficient to substantiate the whole of the claim, the Contractor shall only be entitled to payment for such part of the claim as he has been able to substantiate.

The Engineer shall proceed in accordance with Sub-Clause 3.5 [*Determinations*] to agree or determine (i) the extension (if any) of the Time for Completion (before or after its expiry) in accordance with Sub-Clause 8.4 [*Extension of Time for Completion*], and/or (ii) the additional payment (if any) to which the Contractor is entitled under the Contract.

The requirements of this Sub-Clause are in addition to those of any other Sub-Clause which may apply to a claim. If the Contractor fails to comply with this or another Sub-Clause in relation to any claim, any extension of time and/or additional payment shall take account of the extent (if any) to which the failure has prevented or prejudiced proper investigation of the claim, unless the claim is excluded under the second paragraph of this Sub-Clause.

20.2

Appointment of the Dispute Adjudication Board

Disputes shall be adjudicated by a DAB in accordance with Sub-Clause 20.4 [*Obtaining Dispute Adjudication Board's Decision*]. The Parties shall jointly appoint a DAB by the date stated in the Appendix to Tender.

The DAB shall comprise, as stated in the Appendix to Tender, either one or three suitably qualified persons ("the members"). If the number is not so stated and the Parties do not agree otherwise, the DAB shall comprise three persons.

If the DAB is to comprise three persons, each Party shall nominate one member for the approval of the other Party. The Parties shall consult both these members and shall agree upon the third member, who shall be appointed to act as chairman.

However, if a list of potential members is included in the Contract, the members shall be selected from those on the list, other than anyone who is unable or unwilling to accept appointment to the DAB.

The agreement between the Parties and either the sole member ("adjudicator") or each of the three members shall incorporate by reference the General Conditions of Dispute Adjudication Agreement contained in the Appendix to these General Conditions, with such amendments as are agreed between them.

The terms of the remuneration of either the sole member or each of the three members, including the remuneration of any expert whom the DAB consults, shall be mutually agreed upon by the Parties when agreeing the terms of appointment. Each Party shall be responsible for paying one-half of this remuneration.

If at any time the Parties so agree, they may jointly refer a matter to the DAB for it to give its opinion. Neither Party shall consult the DAB on any matter without the agreement of the other Party.

If at any time the Parties so agree, they may appoint a suitably qualified person or persons to replace (or to be available to replace) any one or more members of the DAB. Unless the Parties agree otherwise, the appointment will come into effect if a member declines to act or is unable to act as a result of death, disability, resignation or termination of appointment.

If any of these circumstances occurs and no such replacement is available, a replacement shall be appointed in the same manner as the replaced person was required to have been nominated or agreed upon, as described in this Sub-Clause.

The appointment of any member may be terminated by mutual agreement of both Parties, but not by the Employer or the Contractor acting alone. Unless otherwise agreed by both Parties, the appointment of the DAB (including each member) shall expire when the discharge referred to in Sub-Clause 14.12 [*Discharge*] shall have become effective.

20.3

Failure to Agree Dispute Adjudication Board

If any of the following conditions apply, namely:

(a)   the Parties fail to agree upon the appointment of the sole member of the DAB by the date stated in the first paragraph of Sub-Clause 20.2,

(b)   either Party fails to nominate a member (for approval by the other Party) of a DAB of three persons by such date,

(c)   the Parties fail to agree upon the appointment of the third member (to act as chairman) of the DAB by such date, or

(d)   the Parties fail to agree upon the appointment of a replacement person within 42 days after the date on which the sole member or one of the three members declines to act or is unable to act as a result of death, disability, resignation or termination of appointment,

then the appointing entity or official named in the Appendix to Tender shall, upon the request of either or both of the Parties and after due consultation with both Parties, appoint this member of the DAB. This appointment shall be final and conclusive. Each Party shall be responsible for paying one-half of the remuneration of the appointing entity or official.

20.4

Obtaining Dispute Adjudication Board's Decision

If a dispute (of any kind whatsoever) arises between the Parties in connection with, or arising out of, the Contract or the execution of the Works, including any dispute as to any certificate, determination, instruction, opinion or valuation of the Engineer, either Party may refer the dispute in writing to the DAB for its decision, with copies to the other Party and the Engineer. Such reference shall state that it is given under this Sub-Clause.

For a DAB of three persons, the DAB shall be deemed to have received such reference on the date when it is received by the chairman of the DAB.

Both Parties shall promptly make available to the DAB all such additional information, further access to the Site, and appropriate facilities, as the DAB may require for the

© FIDIC 1999

Conditions of Contract for Construction

purposes of making a decision on such dispute. The DAB shall be deemed to be not acting as arbitrator(s).

Within 84 days after receiving such reference, or within such other period as may be proposed by the DAB and approved by both Parties, the DAB shall give its decision, which shall be reasoned and shall state that it is given under this Sub-Clause. The decision shall be binding on both Parties, who shall promptly give effect to it unless and until it shall be revised in an amicable settlement or an arbitral award as described below. Unless the Contract has already been abandoned, repudiated or terminated, the Contractor shall continue to proceed with the Works in accordance with the Contract.

If either Party is dissatisfied with the DAB's decision, then either Party may, within 28 days after receiving the decision, give notice to the other Party of its dissatisfaction. If the DAB fails to give its decision within the period of 84 days (or as otherwise approved) after receiving such reference, then either Party may, within 28 days after this period has expired, give notice to the other Party of its dissatisfaction.

In either event, this notice of dissatisfaction shall state that it is given under this Sub-Clause, and shall set out the matter in dispute and the reason(s) for dissatisfaction. Except as stated in Sub-Clause 20.7 [*Failure to Comply with Dispute Adjudication Board's Decision*] and Sub-Clause 20.8 [*Expiry of Dispute Adjudication Board's Appointment*], neither Party shall be entitled to commence arbitration of a dispute unless a notice of dissatisfaction has been given in accordance with this Sub-Clause.

If the DAB has given its decision as to a matter in dispute to both Parties, and no notice of dissatisfaction has been given by either Party within 28 days after it received the DAB's decision, then the decision shall become final and binding upon both Parties.

20.5

Amicable Settlement

Where notice of dissatisfaction has been given under Sub-Clause 20.4 above, both Parties shall attempt to settle the dispute amicably before the commencement of arbitration. However, unless both Parties agree otherwise, arbitration may be commenced on or after the fifty-sixth day after the day on which notice of dissatisfaction was given, even if no attempt at amicable settlement has been made.

20.6

Arbitration

Unless settled amicably, any dispute in respect of which the DAB's decision (if any) has not become final and binding shall be finally settled by international arbitration. Unless otherwise agreed by both Parties:

(a) the dispute shall be finally settled under the Rules of Arbitration of the International Chamber of Commerce,

(b) the dispute shall be settled by three arbitrators appointed in accordance with these Rules, and

(c) the arbitration shall be conducted in the language for communications defined in Sub-Clause 1.4 [*Law and Language*].

The arbitrator(s) shall have full power to open up, review and revise any certificate, determination, instruction, opinion or valuation of the Engineer, and any decision of the DAB, relevant to the dispute. Nothing shall disqualify the Engineer from being called as a witness and giving evidence before the arbitrator(s) on any matter whatsoever relevant to the dispute.

Neither Party shall be limited in the proceedings before the arbitrator(s) to the evidence or arguments previously put before the DAB to obtain its decision, or to the reasons for dissatisfaction given in its notice of dissatisfaction. Any decision of the DAB shall be admissible in evidence in the arbitration.

Arbitration may be commenced prior to or after completion of the Works. The obligations of the Parties, the Engineer and the DAB shall not be altered by reason of any arbitration being conducted during the progress of the Works.

20.7

Failure to Comply with Dispute Adjudication Board's Decision

In the event that:

(a)   neither Party has given notice of dissatisfaction within the period stated in Sub-Clause 20.4 [*Obtaining Dispute Adjudication Board's Decision*],

(b)   the DAB's related decision (if any) has become final and binding, and

(c)   a Party fails to comply with this decision,

then the other Party may, without prejudice to any other rights it may have, refer the failure itself to arbitration under Sub-Clause 20.6 [*Arbitration*]. Sub-Clause 20.4 [*Obtaining Dispute Adjudication Board's Decision*] and Sub-Clause 20.5 [*Amicable Settlement*] shall not apply to this reference.

20.8

Expiry of Dispute Adjudication Board's Appointment

If a dispute arises between the Parties in connection with, or arising out of, the Contract or the execution of the Works and there is no DAB in place, whether by reason of the expiry of the DAB's appointment or otherwise:

(a)   Sub-Clause 20.4 [*Obtaining Dispute Adjudication Board's Decision*] and Sub-Clause 20.5 [*Amicable Settlement*] shall not apply, and

(b)   the dispute may be referred directly to arbitration under Sub-Clause 20.6 [*Arbitration*].

Conditions of Contract for Construction

APPENDIX

General Conditions of Dispute Adjudication Agreement

1

Definitions

Each "Dispute Adjudication Agreement" is a tripartite agreement by and between:
(a)   the "Employer";
(b)   the "Contractor"; and
(c)   the "Member" who is defined in the Dispute Adjudication Agreement as being:
    (i)   the sole member of the "DAB" (or "adjudicator") and, where this is the case, all references to the "Other Members" do not apply, or
    (ii)   one of the three persons who are jointly called the "DAB" (or "dispute adjudication board") and, where this is the case, the other two persons are called the "Other Members".

The Employer and the Contractor have entered (or intend to enter) into a contract, which is called the "Contract" and is defined in the Dispute Adjudication Agreement, which incorporates this Appendix. In the Dispute Adjudication Agreement, words and expressions which are not otherwise defined shall have the meanings assigned to them in the Contract.

2

General Provisions

Unless otherwise stated in the Dispute Adjudication Agreement, it shall take effect on the latest of the following dates:
(a)   the Commencement Date defined in the Contract,
(b)   when the Employer, the Contractor and the Member have each signed the Dispute Adjudication Agreement, or
(c)   when the Employer, the Contractor and each of the Other Members (if any) have respectively each signed a dispute adjudication agreement.

When the Dispute Adjudication Agreement has taken effect, the Employer and the Contractor shall each give notice to the Member accordingly. If the Member does not receive either notice within six months after entering into the Dispute Adjudication Agreement, it shall be void and ineffective.

This employment of the Member is a personal appointment. At any time, the Member may give not less than 70 days' notice of resignation to the Employer and to the Contractor, and the Dispute Adjudication Agreement shall terminate upon the expiry of this period.

No assignment or subcontracting of the Dispute Adjudication Agreement is permitted without the prior written agreement of all the parties to it and of the Other Members (if any).

3

Warranties

The Member warrants and agrees that he/she is and shall be impartial and independent of the Employer, the Contractor and the Engineer. The Member shall promptly disclose, to each of them and to the Other Members (if any), any fact or circumstance which might appear inconsistent with his/her warranty and agreement of impartiality and independence.

When appointing the Member, the Employer and the Contractor relied upon the Member's representations that he/she is:
(a)   experienced in the work which the Contractor is to carry out under the Contract,
(b)   experienced in the interpretation of contract documentation, and
(c)   fluent in the language for communications defined in the Contract.

4

General Obligations of the Member

The Member shall:

(a) have no interest financial or otherwise in the Employer, the Contractor or the Engineer, nor any financial interest in the Contract except for payment under the Dispute Adjudication Agreement;

(b) not previously have been employed as a consultant or otherwise by the Employer, the Contractor or the Engineer, except in such circumstances as were disclosed in writing to the Employer and the Contractor before they signed the Dispute Adjudication Agreement;

(c) have disclosed in writing to the Employer, the Contractor and the Other Members (if any), before entering into the Dispute Adjudication Agreement and to his/her best knowledge and recollection, any professional or personal relationships with any director, officer or employee of the Employer, the Contractor or the Engineer, and any previous involvement in the overall project of which the Contract forms part;

(d) not, for the duration of the Dispute Adjudication Agreement, be employed as a consultant or otherwise by the Employer, the Contractor or the Engineer, except as may be agreed in writing by the Employer, the Contractor and the Other Members (if any);

(e) comply with the annexed procedural rules and with Sub-Clause 20.4 of the Conditions of Contract;

(f) not give advice to the Employer, the Contractor, the Employer's Personnel or the Contractor's Personnel concerning the conduct of the Contract, other than in accordance with the annexed procedural rules;

(g) not while a Member enter into discussions or make any agreement with the Employer, the Contractor or the Engineer regarding employment by any of them, whether as a consultant or otherwise, after ceasing to act under the Dispute Adjudication Agreement;

(h) ensure his/her availability for all site visits and hearings as are necessary;

(i) become conversant with the Contract and with the progress of the Works (and of any other parts of the project of which the Contract forms part) by studying all documents received which shall be maintained in a current working file;

(j) treat the details of the Contract and all the DAB's activities and hearings as private and confidential, and not publish or disclose them without the prior written consent of the Employer, the Contractor and the Other Members (if any); and

(k) be available to give advice and opinions, on any matter relevant to the Contract when requested by both the Employer and the Contractor, subject to the agreement of the Other Members (if any).

5

General Obligations of the Employer and the Contractor

The Employer, the Contractor, the Employer's Personnel and the Contractor's Personnel shall not request advice from or consultation with the Member regarding the Contract, otherwise than in the normal course of the DAB's activities under the Contract and the Dispute Adjudication Agreement, and except to the extent that prior agreement is given by the Employer, the Contractor and the Other Members (if any). The Employer and the Contractor shall be responsible for compliance with this provision, by the Employer's Personnel and the Contractor's Personnel respectively.

The Employer and the Contractor undertake to each other and to the Member that the Member shall not, except as otherwise agreed in writing by the Employer, the Contractor, the Member and the Other Members (if any):

(a) be appointed as an arbitrator in any arbitration under the Contract;

(b) be called as a witness to give evidence concerning any dispute before arbitrator(s) appointed for any arbitration under the Contract; or

(c) be liable for any claims for anything done or omitted in the discharge or purported discharge of the Member's functions, unless the act or omission is shown to have been in bad faith.

Conditions of Contract for Construction

The Employer and the Contractor hereby jointly and severally indemnify and hold the Member harmless against and from claims from which he/she is relieved from liability under the preceding paragraph.

Whenever the Employer or the Contractor refers a dispute to the DAB under Sub-Clause 20.4 of the Conditions of Contract, which will require the Member to make a site visit and attend a hearing, the Employer or the Contractor shall provide appropriate security for a sum equivalent to the reasonable expenses to be incurred by the Member. No account shall be taken of any other payments due or paid to the Member.

6

Payment

The Member shall be paid as follows, in the currency named in the Dispute Adjudication Agreement:

(a) a retainer fee per calendar month, which shall be considered as payment in full for:

   (i) being available on 28 days' notice for all site visits and hearings;

   (ii) becoming and remaining conversant with all project developments and maintaining relevant files;

   (iii) all office and overhead expenses including secretarial services, photocopying and office supplies incurred in connection with his duties; and

   (iv) all services performed hereunder except those referred to in sub-paragraphs (b) and (c) of this Clause.

The retainer fee shall be paid with effect from the last day of the calendar month in which the Dispute Adjudication Agreement becomes effective; until the last day of the calendar month in which the Taking-Over Certificate is issued for the whole of the Works.

With effect from the first day of the calendar month following the month in which Taking-Over Certificate is issued for the whole of the Works, the retainer fee shall be reduced by 50%. This reduced fee shall be paid until the first day of the calendar month in which the Member resigns or the Dispute Adjudication Agreement is otherwise terminated.

(b) a daily fee which shall be considered as payment in full for:

   (i) each day or part of a day up to a maximum of two days' travel time in each direction for the journey between the Member's home and the site, or another location of a meeting with the Other Members (if any);

   (ii) each working day on site visits, hearings or preparing decisions; and

   (iii) each day spent reading submissions in preparation for a hearing.

(c) all reasonable expenses incurred in connection with the Member's duties, including the cost of telephone calls, courier charges, faxes and telexes, travel expenses, hotel and subsistence costs: a receipt shall be required for each item in excess of five percent of the daily fee referred to in sub-paragraph (b) of this Clause;

(d) any taxes properly levied in the Country on payments made to the Member (unless a national or permanent resident of the Country) under this Clause 6.

The retainer and daily fees shall be as specified in the Dispute Adjudication Agreement. Unless it specifies otherwise, these fees shall remain fixed for the first 24 calendar months, and shall thereafter be adjusted by agreement between the Employer, the Contractor and the Member, at each anniversary of the date on which the Dispute Adjudication Agreement became effective.

The Member shall submit invoices for payment of the monthly retainer and air fares quarterly in advance. Invoices for other expenses and for daily fees shall be submitted following the conclusion of a site visit or hearing. All invoices shall be accompanied by a brief description of activities performed during the relevant period and shall be addressed to the Contractor.

The Contractor shall pay each of the Member's invoices in full within 56 calendar days after receiving each invoice and shall apply to the Employer (in the Statements under the Contract) for reimbursement of one-half of the amounts of these invoices. The Employer shall then pay the Contractor in accordance with the Contract.

If the Contractor fails to pay to the Member the amount to which he/she is entitled under the Dispute Adjudication Agreement, the Employer shall pay the amount due to the Member and any other amount which may be required to maintain the operation of the DAB; and without prejudice to the Employer's rights or remedies. In addition to all other rights arising from this default, the Employer shall be entitled to reimbursement of all sums paid in excess of one-half of these payments, plus all costs of recovering these sums and financing charges calculated at the rate specified in Sub-Clause 14.8 of the Conditions of Contract.

If the Member does not receive payment of the amount due within 70 days after submitting a valid invoice, the Member may (i) suspend his/her services (without notice) until the payment is received, and/or (ii) resign his/her appointment by giving notice under Clause 7.

7

Termination

At any time: (i) the Employer and the Contractor may jointly terminate the Dispute Adjudication Agreement by giving 42 days' notice to the Member; or (ii) the Member may resign as provided for in Clause 2.

If the Member fails to comply with the Dispute Adjudication Agreement, the Employer and the Contractor may, without prejudice to their other rights, terminate it by notice to the Member. The notice shall take effect when received by the Member.

If the Employer or the Contractor fails to comply with the Dispute Adjudication Agreement, the Member may, without prejudice to his/her other rights, terminate it by notice to the Employer and the Contractor. The notice shall take effect when received by them both.

Any such notice, resignation and termination shall be final and binding on the Employer, the Contractor and the Member. However, a notice by the Employer or the Contractor, but not by both, shall be of no effect.

8

Default of the Member

If the Member fails to comply with any obligation under Clause 4, he/she shall not be entitled to any fees or expenses hereunder and shall, without prejudice to their other rights, reimburse each of the Employer and the Contractor for any fees and expenses received by the Member and the Other Members (if any), for proceedings or decisions (if any) of the DAB which are rendered void or ineffective.

9

Disputes

Any dispute or claim arising out of or in connection with this Dispute Adjudication Agreement, or the breach, termination or invalidity thereof, shall be finally settled under the Rules of Arbitration of the International Chamber of Commerce by one arbitrator appointed in accordance with these Rules of Arbitration.

 Conditions of Contract for Construction

Annex PROCEDURAL RULES

1   Unless otherwise agreed by the Employer and the Contractor, the DAB shall visit the site at intervals of not more than 140 days, including times of critical construction events, at the request of either the Employer or the Contractor. Unless otherwise agreed by the Employer, the Contractor and the DAB, the period between consecutive visits shall not be less than 70 days, except as required to convene a hearing as described below.

2   The timing of and agenda for each site visit shall be as agreed jointly by the DAB, the Employer and the Contractor, or in the absence of agreement, shall be decided by the DAB. The purpose of site visits is to enable the DAB to become and remain acquainted with the progress of the Works and of any actual or potential problems or claims.

3   Site visits shall be attended by the Employer, the Contractor and the Engineer and shall be co-ordinated by the Employer in co-operation with the Contractor. The Employer shall ensure the provision of appropriate conference facilities and secretarial and copying services. At the conclusion of each site visit and before leaving the site, the DAB shall prepare a report on its activities during the visit and shall send copies to the Employer and the Contractor.

4   The Employer and the Contractor shall furnish to the DAB one copy of all documents which the DAB may request, including Contract documents, progress reports, variation instructions, certificates and other documents pertinent to the performance of the Contract. All communications between the DAB and the Employer or the Contractor shall be copied to the other Party. If the DAB comprises three persons, the Employer and the Contractor shall send copies of these requested documents and these communications to each of these persons.

5   If any dispute is referred to the DAB in accordance with Sub-Clause 20.4 of the Conditions of Contract, the DAB shall proceed in accordance with Sub-Clause 20.4 and these Rules. Subject to the time allowed to give notice of a decision and other relevant factors, the DAB shall:

(a)   act fairly and impartially as between the Employer and the Contractor, giving each of them a reasonable opportunity of putting his case and responding to the other's case, and

(b)   adopt procedures suitable to the dispute, avoiding unnecessary delay or expense.

6   The DAB may conduct a hearing on the dispute, in which event it will decide on the date and place for the hearing and may request that written documentation and arguments from the Employer and the Contractor be presented to it prior to or at the hearing.

7   Except as otherwise agreed in writing by the Employer and the Contractor, the DAB shall have power to adopt an inquisitorial procedure, to refuse admission to hearings or audience at hearings to any persons other than representatives of the Employer, the Contractor and the Engineer, and to proceed in the absence of any party who the DAB is satisfied received notice of the hearing; but shall have discretion to decide whether and to what extent this power may be exercised.

8   The Employer and the Contractor empower the DAB, among other things, to:

(a)   establish the procedure to be applied in deciding a dispute,

(b)   decide upon the DAB's own jurisdiction, and as to the scope of any dispute referred to it,

(c)   conduct any hearing as it thinks fit, not being bound by any rules or procedures other than those contained in the Contract and these Rules,

(d)   take the initiative in ascertaining the facts and matters required for a decision,

(e)   make use of its own specialist knowledge, if any,

(f)   decide upon the payment of financing charges in accordance with the Contract,

(g)   decide upon any provisional relief such as interim or conservatory measures, and

(h)   open up, review and revise any certificate, decision, determination, instruction, opinion or valuation of the Engineer, relevant to the dispute.

9   The DAB shall not express any opinions during any hearing concerning the merits of any arguments advanced by the Parties. Thereafter, the DAB shall make and give its decision in accordance with Sub-Clause 20.4, or as otherwise agreed by the Employer and the Contractor in writing. If the DAB comprises three persons:

(a)   it shall convene in private after a hearing, in order to have discussions and prepare its decision;

(b)   it shall endeavour to reach a unanimous decision: if this proves impossible the applicable decision shall be made by a majority of the Members, who may require the minority Member to prepare a written report for submission to the Employer and the Contractor; and

(c)   if a Member fails to attend a meeting or hearing, or to fulfil any required function, the other two Members may nevertheless proceed to make a decision, unless:

    (i)   either the Employer or the Contractor does not agree that they do so, or

    (ii)   the absent Member is the chairman and he/she instructs the other Members to not make a decision.

INDEX OF SUB-CLAUSES

© FIDIC 1999   Conditions of Contract for Construction

GENERAL CONDITIONS

GUIDANCE

FORMS

© FIDIC 1999

Conditions of Contract for Construction

GENERAL CONDITIONS

GUIDANCE

FORMS

© FIDIC 1999   Conditions of Contract for Construction

GENERAL CONDITIONS

GUIDANCE FOR THE
PREPARATION OF
PARTICULAR CONDITIONS

FORMS OF LETTER OF
TENDER, CONTRACT
AGREEMENT AND
DISPUTE ADJUDICATION
AGREEMENT

FIDIC® Conditions of Contract
for CONSTRUCTION

FOR BUILDING AND ENGINEERING WORKS
DESIGNED BY THE EMPLOYER

Guidance for the Preparation of Particular
Conditions

FEDERATION INTERNATIONALE DES INGENIEURS-CONSEILS
INTERNATIONAL FEDERATION OF CONSULTING ENGINEERS
INTERNATIONALE VEREINIGUNG BERATENDER INGENIEURE
FEDERACION INTERNACIONAL DE INGENIEROS CONSULTORES

FIDIC

Guidance
for the Preparation of Particular Conditions

CONTENTS

Guidance for the Preparation of Particular Conditions

INTRODUCTION

The terms of the Conditions of Contract for Construction have been prepared by the Fédération Internationale des Ingénieurs-Conseils (FIDIC) and are recommended for general use for the purpose of the construction (excluding most design) of building or engineering works where tenders are invited on an international basis. Modifications to the Conditions may be required in some legal jurisdictions, particularly if they are to be used on domestic contracts.

Under the usual arrangements for this type of contract, the Contractor constructs the works in accordance with design details provided by the Employer or his representative, the Engineer. Although these Conditions allow for the possibility that the Contractor may be required to design parts of the permanent works, they are not intended for use where most of the works are designed by the Contractor. For these Works, it would be more appropriate to utilise FIDIC's Conditions of Contract for Plant and Design-Build or Conditions of Contract for EPC/Turnkey Projects.

The guidance hereafter is intended to assist writers of the Particular Conditions by giving options for various sub-clauses where appropriate. As far as possible, example wording is included, between lines. In some cases, however, only an aide-memoire is given.

Before incorporating any example wording, it must be checked to ensure that it is wholly suitable for the particular circumstances. Unless it is considered suitable, example wording should be amended before use.

Where example wording is amended, and in all cases where other amendments or additions are made, care must be taken to ensure that no ambiguity is created, either with the General Conditions or between the clauses in the Particular Conditions.

In the preparation of the Conditions of Contract to be included in the tender documents for a contract, the following text can be used:

> The Conditions of Contract comprise the "General Conditions", which form part of the "Conditions of Contract for Construction" First Edition 1999 published by the Fédération Internationale des Ingénieurs-Conseils (FIDIC), and the following "Particular Conditions", which include amendments and additions to such General Conditions.

There are no Sub-Clauses in the General Conditions which require data to be included in the Particular Conditions. As noted in sub-paragraph (ii) of the Foreword, the General Conditions refer to any necessary data being contained in the Appendix to Tender or (for technical matters) in the Specification.

FIDIC has published a document entitled "Tendering Procedure" which presents a systematic approach to the selection of tenderers and the obtaining and evaluation of tenders; the second edition was published in 1994. The document is intended to assist the Employer to receive sound competitive tenders with a minimum of qualifications. FIDIC intends to update Tendering Procedure and to publish a guide to the use of these Conditions of Contract for Construction.

Notes on the Preparation of Tender Documents

The tender documents should be prepared by suitably-qualified engineers who are familiar with the technical aspects of the required works, and a review by suitably-qualified lawyers may be advisable. The tender documents issued to tenderers will consist of the Conditions of Contract, the Specification, the Drawings, and the Letter of Tender and Schedules for completion by the Tenderer. For this type of contract, where the Works are valued by measurement, the Bill of Quantities will usually be the most important Schedule. A Daywork Schedule may also be necessary, to cover minor works to be evaluated at cost. In addition, each of the Tenderers should receive the data referred to in Sub-Clause 4.10, and the Instructions to Tenderers to advise them of any special matters which the Employer wishes them to take into account when pricing the Bill of Quantities but which are not to form part of the Contract. When the Employer accepts the Letter of Tender, the Contract (which then comes into full force and effect) includes these completed Schedules.

The Specification may include the matters referred to in some or all of the following Sub-Clauses:

1.8	Requirements for Contractor's Documents
1.13	Permissions being obtained by the Employer
2.1	Phased possession of foundations, structures, plant or means of access
4.1	Contractor's designs
4.6	Other contractors (and others) on the Site
4.7	Setting-out points, lines and levels of reference
4.14	Third parties
4.18	Environmental constraints
4.19	Electricity, water, gas and other services available on the Site
4.20	Employer's Equipment and free-issue material
5.1	Nominated Subcontractors
6.6	Facilities for Personnel
7.2	Samples
7.4	Testing during manufacture and/or construction
9.1	Tests on Completion
13.5	Provisional Sums

Many Sub-Clauses in the General Conditions make reference to data being contained in the Appendix to Tender, providing a convenient location for the data which is usually required. The example form in this publication thus provides a check-list of the data required; but there is no indication, either in the General Conditions or in the example Appendix to Tender, that this data is either prescribed by the Employer or inserted by the Tenderer. The Employer should prepare the Appendix to Tender, based on this example form, with the elements completed to the extent of his requirements.

The Employer may also require other data from Tenderers, and include a questionnaire in the Schedules.

The Instructions to Tenderers may need to specify any constraints on the completion of the Appendix to Tender and/or Schedules, and/or specify the extent of other information which each Tenderer is to include with his Tender. If each Tenderer is to produce a parent company guarantee and/or a tender security, these requirements (which apply prior to the Contract becoming effective) should be included in the Instructions to Tenderers: example forms are annexed to this document as Annexes A and B. The Instructions may include matters referred to in some or all of the following Sub-Clauses:

4.3	Contractor's Representative (name and curriculum vitae)
4.9	Quality Assurance system
9.1	Tests on Completion
18	Insurances
20	Resolution of disputes

3

Clause 1   General Provisions

Sub-Clause 1.1   Definitions

It may be necessary to amend some of the definitions. For example:

1.1.3.1	the Base Date could be defined as a particular calendar date
1.1.4.6	one particular Foreign Currency may be required by the financing institution
1.1.4.8	a different currency may be required to be the contract Local Currency
1.1.6.2	the references to "Country" may be inappropriate for a cross-border Site

Sub-Clause 1.2   Interpretation

If the references to "profit" are to be more precisely specified, this Sub-Clause may be varied:

EXAMPLE   At the end of Sub-Clause 1.2, insert:

In these Conditions, provisions including the expression "Cost plus reasonable profit" require this profit to be one-twentieth (5%) of this Cost.

Sub-Clause 1.5   Priority of Documents

An order of precedence is usually necessary, in case a conflict is subsequently found among the contract documents. If no order of precedence is to be prescribed, this Sub-Clause may be varied:

EXAMPLE   Delete Sub-Clause 1.5 and substitute:

The documents forming the Contract are to be taken as mutually explanatory of one another. If an ambiguity or discrepancy is found, the priority shall be such as may be accorded by the governing law. The Engineer has authority to issue any instruction which he considers necessary to resolve an ambiguity or discrepancy.

Sub-Clause 1.6   Contract Agreement

The form of Agreement should be included in the tender documents as an annex to the Particular Conditions: an example form is included at the end of this publication. If lengthy tender negotiations were necessary, it may be considered advisable for the Contract Agreement to record the Accepted Contract Amount, Base Date and/or Commencement Date. Entry into an Agreement may be necessary under applicable law.

Sub-Clause 1.14   Joint and Several Liability

For a major contract, detailed requirements for the joint venture may need to be specified. For example, it may be desirable for each member to produce a parent company guarantee: an example form is annexed to this document as Annex A.

These requirements, which apply prior to the Contract becoming effective, should be included in the Instructions to Tenderers. The Employer will wish the leader of the joint venture to be appointed at an early stage, providing a single point of contact thereafter, and will not wish to be involved in a dispute between the members of a joint venture. The Employer should scrutinise the joint venture agreement carefully, and it may have to be approved by the project's financing institutions.

Additional Sub-Clause   Details to be Confidential

If confidentiality is required, an additional sub-clause may be added:

EXAMPLE SUB-CLAUSE

The Contractor shall treat the details of the Contract as private and confidential, except to the extent necessary to carry out obligations under it or to comply with applicable Laws. The Contractor shall not publish, permit to be published, or disclose any particulars of the Works in any trade or technical paper or elsewhere without the previous agreement of the Employer.

Clause 2   The Employer

Sub-Clause 2.1   Right of Access to the Site

If right of access cannot be granted, both early and thereafter exclusively, details should be given in the Specification.

Sub-Clause 2.3   Employer's Personnel

These provisions should be reflected in the Employer's contracts with any other contractors on the Site.

Clause 3   The Engineer

Sub-Clause 3.1   Engineer's Duties and Authority

Any requirements for Employer's approval should be set out in the Particular Conditions:

EXAMPLE

The Engineer shall obtain the specific approval of the Employer before taking action under the following Sub-Clauses of these Conditions:

(a)   Sub-Clause _____ **

(b)   Sub-Clause _____ **

** (insert number; describe action, unless all require approval)

This list should be extended or reduced as necessary. If the obligation to obtain the approval of the Employer only applies beyond certain limits, financial or otherwise, the example wording should be varied.

Additional Sub-Clause   Management Meetings

EXAMPLE SUB-CLAUSE

The Engineer or the Contractor's Representative may require the other to attend a management meeting in order to review the arrangements for future work. The Engineer shall record the business of management meetings and supply copies of the record to those attending the meeting and to the Employer. In the record, responsibilities for any actions to be taken shall be in accordance with the Contract.

Clause 4   The Contractor

Sub-Clause 4.1   Contractor's General Obligations

Occasionally, there may be an item of Temporary Works for which the Contractor will not be fully responsible. For example, the Contract may specify temporary arrangements for river diversion which have been designed by the Engineer. In these cases, the Sub-Clause may require amendment, taking account of the type of this item of Temporary Works, and of the extent of the Employer's responsibility.

Sub-Clause 4.2   Performance Security

The acceptable form(s) of Performance Security should be included in the tender documents, annexed to the Particular Conditions. Example forms are annexed to this document as Annex C and Annex D. They incorporate two sets of Uniform Rules published by the International Chamber of Commerce (the "ICC", which is based at 38 Cours Albert 1er, 75008 Paris, France), which also publishes guides to these Uniform Rules. These example forms and the wording of the Sub-Clause may have to be amended to comply with applicable law.

EXAMPLE   At the end of the second paragraph of Sub-Clause 4.2, insert:

If the Performance Security is in the form of a bank guarantee, it shall be issued either (a) by a bank located in the Country, or (b) directly by a foreign bank acceptable to the Employer. If the Performance Security is not in the form of a bank guarantee, it shall be furnished by a financial entity registered, or licensed to do business, in the Country.

Sub-Clause 4.3   Contractor's Representative

If the Representative is known at the time of submission of the Tender, the Tenderer may propose the Representative. The Tenderer may wish to propose alternatives, especially if the contract award seems likely to be delayed. If the ruling language is not the same as the language for day to day communications (under Sub-Clause 1.4), or if for any other reason it is necessary to stipulate that the Contractor's Representative shall be fluent in a particular language, one of the following sentences may be added.

EXAMPLE   At the end of Sub-Clause 4.3, add:

The Contractor's Representative and all these persons shall also be fluent in _____ (insert name of language)

EXAMPLE   At the end of Sub-Clause 4.3, add:

If the Contractor's Representative, or these persons, is not fluent in _____ (insert name of language), the Contractor shall make a competent interpreter available during all working hours.

Sub-Clause 4.4   Subcontractors

The wording in the General Conditions includes the conditions which will usually be applicable. If less (or no) consent is required, some (or all) of sub-paragraphs (a) to (d) may be deleted, or qualified in the Particular Conditions:

EXAMPLE	Prior consent shall not be required if the value of the subcontract is less than 0.01% of the Accepted Contract Amount.

A sentence may be added to increase the extent to which consent is required:

EXAMPLE	The prior consent of the Engineer shall be obtained to the suppliers of the following Materials: (insert details: for example, specific manufactured or prefabricated items)

A sentence may be added in order to encourage the Contractor to use local contractors:

EXAMPLE	Where practicable, the Contractor shall give a fair and reasonable opportunity for contractors from the Country to be appointed as Sub-contractors.

Sub-Clause 4.8   Safety Procedures

If the Contractor is sharing occupation of the Site with others, it may not be appropriate for him to provide some of the listed items. In these circumstances, the Employer's obligations should be specified.

Sub-Clause 4.9   Quality Assurance

The wording in the General Conditions imposes the requirement of a quality assurance system in accordance with details specified in the Contract. If inappropriate, this Sub-Clause may be deleted.

Sub-Clause 4.12   Unforeseeable Physical Conditions

In the case of major sub-surface works, the allocation of the risk of sub-surface conditions is an aspect which should be considered when tender documents are being prepared. If this risk is to be shared between the parties, the Sub-Clause may be amended:

EXAMPLE	Delete sub-paragraph (b) of Sub-Clause 4.12 and substitute:
	(b) payment for any such Cost, _____ per cent (_____ %) of which shall be included in the Contract Price (the balance _____ percent of the Cost shall be borne by the Contractor).

Sub-Clause 4.17   Contractor's Equipment

If the Contractor is not to provide all the Contractor's Equipment necessary to complete the Works, the Employer's obligations should be specified: see Sub-Clause 4.20. If vesting of Contractor's Equipment is required, further paragraphs may be added, subject to their being consistent with applicable laws:

EXAMPLE	At the end of Sub-Clause 4.17, add the following paragraphs: Contractor's Equipment which is owned by the Contractor (either directly or indirectly) shall be deemed to be the property of the Employer with effect from its arrival on the Site. This vesting of property shall not:

(a)   affect the responsibility or liability of the Employer,

(b)   prejudice the right of the Contractor to the sole use of the vested Contractor's Equipment for the purpose of the Works, or

(c)   affect the Contractor's responsibility to operate and maintain Contractor's Equipment.

The property in each item shall be deemed to revest in the Contractor when he is entitled either to remove it from the Site or to receive the Taking-Over Certificate for the Works, whichever occurs first.

Sub-Clause 4.19   Electricity, Water and Gas

If services are to be available for the Contractor to use, the Specification should give details, including locations and prices.

Sub-Clause 4.20   Employer's Equipment and Free-Issue Material

For this Sub-Clause to apply, the Specification should describe each item which the Employer will provide and/or operate and should specify all necessary details. With some types of facilities, further provisions may be necessary, in order to clarify aspects such as liability and insurance.

Sub-Clause 4.22   Security of the Site

If the Contractor is sharing occupation of the Site with others, it may not be appropriate for him to be responsible for its security. In these circumstances, the Employer's obligations should be specified.

Clause 5   Nominated Subcontractors

In most cases under Sub-Clause 4.4, the Contractor selects Subcontractors, subject to any constraints specified in the Contract. Clause 5 provides for the particular situation whereby the Employer may select a Subcontractor, although the second sentence of Sub-Clause 4.4 should still apply.

The sub-paragraphs of Sub-Clause 5.2 indicate some of the problems which may have to be overcome.

If a nominated Subcontractor is to be required, full details should be included in the tender documents. If the Employer anticipates that a Subcontractor is to be instructed under Clause 13 but is not to be a nominated Subcontractor, Clause 5 should be amended, describing the particular circumstances.

Clause 6   Staff and Labour

Sub-Clause 6.5   Working Hours

If the Employer does not wish to specify working hours in the Appendix to Tender, or to restrict them to the times specified by the Tenderer (in order to plan the Engineer's supervision, for example), this Sub-Clause may be deleted.

Sub-Clause 6.6   Facilities for Staff and Labour

If the Employer will make some accommodation available, his obligations to do so should be specified.

Sub-Clause 6.8   Contractor's Superintendence

If the ruling language is not the same as the language for day to day communications (under Sub-Clause 1.4), or if for any other reason it is necessary to stipulate that the Contractor's superintending staff shall be fluent in a particular language, the following sentence may be added.

EXAMPLE

Insert at the end of Sub-Clause 6.8:

A reasonable proportion of the Contractor's superintending staff shall have a working knowledge of

(insert name of language),

or the Contractor shall have a sufficient number of competent interpreters available on Site during all working hours.

Additional Sub-Clauses

It may be necessary to add a few sub-clauses to take account of the circumstances and locality of the Site:

EXAMPLE SUB-CLAUSE

Foreign Staff and Labour

The Contractor may import any personnel who are necessary for the execution of the Works. The Contractor must ensure that these personnel are provided with the required residence visas and work permits. The Contractor shall be responsible for the return to the place where they were recruited or to their domicile of imported Contractor's Personnel. In the event of the death in the Country of any of these personnel or members of their families, the Contractor shall similarly be responsible for making the appropriate arrangements for their return or burial.

EXAMPLE SUB-CLAUSE

Measures against Insect and Pest Nuisance

The Contractor shall at all times take the necessary precautions to protect all staff and labour employed on the Site from insect and pest nuisance, and to reduce their danger to health. The Contractor shall provide suitable prophylactics for the Contractor's Personnel and shall comply with all the regulations of the local health authorities, including use of appropriate insecticide.

EXAMPLE SUB-CLAUSE

Alcoholic Liquor or Drugs

The Contractor shall not, otherwise than in accordance with the Laws of the Country, import, sell, give, barter or otherwise dispose of any alcoholic liquor or drugs, or permit or allow importation, sale, gift, barter or disposal by Contractor's Personnel.

EXAMPLE SUB-CLAUSE

Arms and Ammunition

The Contractor shall not give, barter or otherwise dispose of to any person, any arms or ammunition of any kind, or allow Contractor's Personnel to do so.

EXAMPLE SUB-CLAUSE

Festivals and Religious Customs

The Contractor shall respect the Country's recognised festivals, days of rest and religious or other customs.

Clause 7   Plant, Materials and Workmanship

Additional Sub-Clause

If the Contract is being financed by an institution whose rules or policies require a restriction on the use of its funds, a further sub-clause may be added:

EXAMPLE SUB-CLAUSE

All Goods shall have their origin in eligible source countries as defined in

(insert name of published guidelines for procurement).

Goods shall be transported by carriers from these eligible source countries, unless exempted by the Employer in writing on the basis of potential excessive costs or delays. Surety, insurance and banking services shall be provided by insurers and bankers from the eligible source countries.

Clause 8   Commencement, Delays and Suspension

Sub-Clause 8.2   Time for Completion

If the Works are to be taken-over in stages, these stages should be defined as Sections, in the Appendix to Tender.

Sub-Clause 8.7   Delay Damages

Under many legal systems, the amount of these pre-defined damages must represent a reasonable pre-estimate of the Employer's probable loss in the event of delay. If the Accepted Contract Amount is to be quoted as the sum of figures in more than one currency, it may be preferable to define these damages (per day) as the percentage reduction which would be applied to each of these figures. If the Accepted Contract Amount is expressed in the Local Currency, the damages per day may either be defined as a percentage or be defined as a figure in Local Currency: see Sub-Clause 14.15(b).

Additional Sub-Clause

Incentives for early completion may be included in the tender documents (although Sub-Clause 13.2 refers to accelerated completion):

Sections are required to be completed by the dates given in the Appendix to Tender in order that these Sections may be occupied and used by the Employer in advance of the completion of the whole of the Works. Details of the work required to be executed to entitle the Contractor to bonus payments and the amount of the bonuses are stated in the Specification.

For the purposes of calculating bonus payments, the dates given in the Appendix to Tender for completion of Sections are fixed. No adjustments of the dates by reason of granting an extension of the Time for Completion will be allowed.

Clause 9   Tests on Completion

Sub-Clause 9.1   Contractor's Obligations

The Specification should describe the tests which the Contractor is to carry out before being entitled to a Taking-Over Certificate. If the Works are to be tested and taken-over in stages, the tests requirements may have to take account of the effect of some parts of the Works being incomplete.

Clause 10   Employer's Taking Over

Sub-Clause 10.1   Taking-Over Certificate

If the Works are to be taken-over in stages, these stages should be defined as Sections, in the Appendix to Tender. Precise geographical definitions are advisable, and the Appendix should include a table, so as to define the Time for Completion and delay damages: the table is shown in the example Appendix.

Clause 11   Defects Liability

Sub-Clause 11.10   Unfulfilled Obligations

It may be necessary to review this Sub-Clause in relation to the period of liability under the applicable law.

Clause 12   Measurement and Evaluation

Sub-Clause 12.1   Works to be Measured

If any part of the Permanent Works is to be measured according to records of its construction, details should be specified in the tender documents, including any records for which the Contractor is to be responsible.

Clause 13   Variations and Adjustments

Variations can be initiated by any of three ways:

(a) the Engineer may instruct the variation under Sub-Clause 13.1, without prior agreement as to feasibility or price;

(b) the Contractor may initiate his own proposals under Sub-Clause 13.2, which are intended to benefit both Parties; or

(c) the Engineer may request a proposal under Sub-Clause 13.3, seeking prior agreement so as to minimise dispute.

Sub-Clause 13.8   Adjustments for Changes in Cost

These provisions for adjustments may be required if it would be unreasonable for the Contractor to bear the risk of escalating costs due to inflation. Unless this Sub-Clause is not to apply, the Appendix to Tender should include a table for each of the currencies of payment: the appropriate table is shown in the example Appendix. Particular care should be taken in the calculation of the weightings/coefficients ("a", "b", "c", ..., the total of which must not exceed unity) and in the selection and verification of cost indices. Expert advice may be appropriate.

Clause 14   Contract Price and Payment

Sub-Clause 14.1   The Contract Price

When writing the Particular Conditions, consideration should be given to the amount and timing of payment(s) to the Contractor. A positive cash flow is clearly of benefit to the Contractor, and tenderers will take account of the interim payment procedures when preparing their tenders.

Additional Sub-Clauses may be required to cover any exceptions to the options set out in Sub-Clause 14.1, and any other matters relating to payment.

Cost-plus contracts, under which the actual Costs are determined and paid, are unusual and only used when (for reasons of urgency or otherwise) the Employer is willing to accept the risks involved. If the Contractor is to be paid actual Costs, Clause 12 should be replaced by provisions describing the method of determining the Costs and Contract Price. As a result, the provisions in the General Conditions which entitle the Contractor to payment of additional Costs will generally be of no effect.

Sub-Clause 14.1(a) would not apply if payment is to be made on a lump sum basis.

Lump sum contracts may be suitable if the tender documents include details which are sufficiently complete for construction and for Variations to be unlikely. From the information supplied in the tender documents, the Contractor can prepare any other details necessary, and construct the Works, without having to refer back to the Engineer for clarification or further information.

Further design by the Contractor (under sub-paragraphs (a) to (d) of Sub-Clause 4.1) is not precluded. However, these Conditions would be inappropriate if significant design input by the Contractor is required. In those cases, FIDIC's other forms may be more appropriate: see FIDIC's Conditions of Contract for Plant and Design-Build or Conditions of Contract for EPC/Turnkey Projects.

For a lump sum contract, the tender documents should include a schedule of payments (see Sub-Clause 14.4), and any drawings required for construction may be specified as being Contractor's Documents. The Specification should describe the procedures under which the Contractor submits these Documents for the Engineer to approve.

EXAMPLE PROVISIONS FOR A LUMP SUM CONTRACT

Delete Clause 12.

Delete the last sentence of Sub-Clause 13.3 and substitute:

Upon instructing or approving a Variation, the Engineer shall proceed in accordance with Sub-Clause 3.5 to agree or determine adjustments to the Contract Price and to the schedule of payments under Sub-Clause 14.4. These adjustments shall include reasonable profit, and shall take account of the Contractor's submissions under Sub-Clause 13.2 if applicable.

Delete sub-paragraph (a) of Sub-Clause 14.1 and substitute:

(a)   the Contract Price shall be the lump sum Accepted Contract Amount and be subject to adjustments in accordance with the Contract;

If Sub-Clause 14.1(b) is not to apply, additional Sub-Clause(s) should be added.

EXAMPLE SUB-CLAUSE ON EXEMPTION FROM DUTIES

All Goods imported by the Contractor into the Country shall be exempt from customs and other import duties, if the Employer's prior written approval is obtained for import. The Employer shall endorse the necessary exemption documents prepared by the Contractor for presentation in order to clear the Goods through Customs, and shall also provide the following exemption documents:

(describe the necessary documents, which the Contractor will be unable to prepare)

If exemption is not then granted, the customs duties payable and paid shall be reimbursed by the Employer.

All imported Goods, which are not incorporated in or expended in connection with the Works, shall be exported on completion of the Contract. If not exported, the Goods will be assessed for duties as applicable to the Goods involved in accordance with the Laws of the Country.

However, exemption may not available for:

(a)   Goods which are similar to those locally produced, unless they are not available in sufficient quantities or are of a different standard to that which is necessary for the Works; and

(b)   any element of duty or tax inherent in the price of goods or services procured in the Country, which shall be deemed to be included in the Accepted Contract Amount.

Port dues, quay dues and, except as set out above, any element of tax or duty inherent in the price of goods or services shall be deemed to be included in the Accepted Contract Amount.

EXAMPLE SUB-CLAUSE ON EXEMPTION FROM TAXES

Expatriate (foreign) personnel shall not be liable for income tax levied in the Country on earnings paid in any foreign currency, or for income tax levied on subsistence, rentals and similar services directly furnished by the Contractor to Contractor's Personnel, or for allowances in lieu. If any Contractor's Personnel have part of their earnings paid in the Country in a foreign currency, they may export (after the conclusion of their term of service on the Works) any balance remaining of their earnings paid in foreign currencies.

The Employer shall seek exemption for the purposes of this Sub-Clause. If it is not granted, the relevant taxes paid shall be reimbursed by the Employer.

Sub-Clause 14.2   Advance Payment

When writing the Particular Conditions, consideration should be given to the benefits of advance payment(s). Unless this Sub-Clause is not to apply, the total advance payment (and the number of instalments if more than one) must be specified in the Appendix to Tender. The rate of deduction for the repayments should be checked to ensure that repayment is achieved before completion. The typical figures in sub-paragraphs (a) and (b) of the General Conditions Sub-Clause are based on the assumption that the total advance payment is less than 22% of the Accepted Contract Amount.

The acceptable form(s) of guarantee should be included in the tender documents, annexed to the Particular Conditions: an example form is annexed to this document, as Annex E.

Sub-Clause 14.7   Payment

If a different period for payment is to apply, the Sub-Clause may be amended:

EXAMPLE

In sub-paragraph (b) of Sub-Clause 14.7, delete "56" and substitute "42"

If the country/countries of payment need to be specified, details may be included in a Schedule.

Sub-Clause 14.8   Delayed Payment

If the discount rate of the central bank in the country of the currency of payment is not a reasonable basis for assessing the Contractor's financing costs, a new rate may have to be defined. Alternatively, the actual financing Costs could be paid, taking account of local financing arrangements.

Sub-Clause 14.9   Payment of Retention Money

If part of the Retention Money is to be released and substituted by an appropriate guarantee, an additional Sub-Clause may be added. The acceptable form(s) of guarantee should be included in the tender documents, annexed to the Particular Conditions: an example form is annexed to this document, as Annex F.

EXAMPLE SUB-CLAUSE FOR RELEASE OF RETENTION

When the Retention Money has reached three-fifths (60%) of the limit of Retention Money stated in the Appendix to Tender, the Engineer shall certify and the Employer shall make payment of half (50%) of the limit of Retention Money to the Contractor if he obtains a guarantee, in a form and provided by an entity approved by the Employer, in amounts and currencies equal to the payment.

The Contractor shall ensure that the guarantee is valid and enforceable until the Contractor has executed and completed the Works and remedied any defects, as specified for the Performance Security in Sub-Clause 4.2, and shall be returned to the Contractor accordingly. This release of retention shall be in lieu of the release of the second half of the Retention Money under the second paragraph of Sub-Clause 14.9.

Sub-Clause 14.15   Currencies of Payment

If all payments are to be made in Local Currency, it must be named in the Letter of Tender, and only the first sentence of this Sub-Clause will apply. Alternatively, the Sub-Clause may then be replaced:

EXAMPLE SUB-CLAUSE FOR A SINGLE CURRENCY CONTRACT

The currency of account shall be the Local Currency and all payments made in accordance with the Contract shall be in Local Currency. The Local Currency payments shall be fully convertible, except those for local costs. The percentage attributed to local costs shall be as stated in the Appendix to Tender.

Financing Arrangements

For major contracts in some markets, there may be a need to secure finance from entities such as aid agencies, development banks, export credit agencies, or other international financing institutions. If financing is to be procured from any of these sources, the Particular Conditions may need to incorporate its special requirements. The exact wording will depend on the relevant institution, so reference will need to be made to them to ascertain their requirements, and to seek approval of the draft tender documents.

These requirements may include tendering procedures which need to be adopted in order to render the eventual contract eligible for financing, and/or special Sub-Clauses which may need to be incorporated into the Particular Conditions. The following examples indicate some of the topics which the institution's requirements may cover:

(a)   prohibition from discrimination against the shipping companies of any one country;

(b)   ensuring that the Contract is subject to a widely-accepted neutral law;

(c)   provision for arbitration under recognised international rules and at a neutral location;

(d)   giving the Contractor the right to suspend/terminate in the event of default under the financing arrangements;

(e)   restricting the right to reject Plant;

(f)   specifying the payments due in the event of termination;

(g)   specifying that the Contract does not become effective until certain conditions precedent have been satisfied, including pre-disbursement conditions for the financing arrangements; and

(h)   obliging the Employer to make payments from his own resources if, for any reason, the funds under the financing arrangements are insufficient to meet the payments due to the Contractor, whether due to a default under the financing arrangements or otherwise.

In addition, the financing institution or bank may wish the Contract to include references to the financing arrangements, especially if funding from more than one source is to be arranged to finance different elements of supply. It is not unusual for the Particular Conditions to include special provisions identifying different categories of Plant and specifying the documents to be presented to the relevant financing institution to obtain payment. If the financing institution's requirements are not met, it may be difficult (or even impossible) to secure suitable financing for the project, and/or the institution may decline to provide finance for part or all of the Contract.

However, where the financing is not tied to the export of goods and services from any particular country but is simply provided by commercial banks lending to the Employer, those banks may be concerned to ensure that the Contractor's rights are very restricted. These banks may wish the Contract to exclude any reference to the financing arrangements, and/or to restrict the Contractor's rights under Clause 16.

FORM OF SUB-CLAUSE WHICH A FINANCING INSTITUTION MAY REQUIRE

The Accepted Contract Amount is made up as follows:

(breakdown into items and/or into supply/delivery/etc)

and shall be payable by the Employer to the Contractor as set out below.

(a) _____ % of the Accepted Contract Amount shall be payable by a direct payment from the Employer to the Contractor within 28 days of receipt by the Employer of the following documents:

    (i) commercial invoice addressed to the Employer specifying the amount of the payment now due,
    (ii) advance payment security guarantee issued by _____ Bank in the form annexed,
    (iii) performance security guarantee issued by _____ Bank in the form annexed, and
    (iv) Interim Payment Certificate confirming the payment due and specifying the amount.

(b) _____ % of the contract price for the supply of Plant shall be payable as follows:

    (i) _____ % of the estimated contract value of the Plant supplied, by direct payment from the Employer to the Contractor on shipment of each item, against the following documents:
        (original) commercial invoice,
        (original) shipping documents,
        (original) certificate of origin,
        (original) insurance certificate, and
        (original) Interim Payment Certificate confirming the payment due and specifying the amount.

    (ii) _____ % of the estimated contract value of the Plant supplied, by disbursement from the Loan Agreement to the Contractor on shipment of each item, on presentation of a Qualifying Certificate in the form annexed and copies of the documents listed in sub-paragraph (b)(i) above.

(c) the balance of the Contract Price shall be payable as follows:

    (i) _____ % of the estimated contract value of the services rendered, by direct payment from the Employer to the Contractor on execution of the relevant service, against the following documents:

(original) commercial invoice, and
(original) Interim Payment Certificate confirming the payment due and specifying the amount.

(ii) _____ % of the estimated contract value of the services rendered, by disbursement from the Loan Agreement to the Contractor, on presentation of a Qualifying Certificate in the form annexed and copies of the documents listed in sub-paragraph (c)(i) above.

(d) The direct payments by the Employer specified in sub-paragraph (b) shall be made by an irrevocable letter of credit established by the Employer in favour of the Contractor and confirmed by a bank acceptable to the Contractor.

The above arrangements (involving financing institution(s), Employer and Contractor) may be initiated by the Employer; or by the Contractor, before submitting the Tender. Alternatively, the Contractor may be prepared to initiate financing arrangements and retain responsibility for them, although he would probably be unable or unwilling to provide finance from his own resources. His financing bank's requirements would then affect his attitude in contract negotiations. They might well require the Employer to make interim payments, although a large proportion of the Contract Price might be withheld until the Works are complete.

This payment arrangement can be achieved either by a high Percentage of Retention; or by a suitably completed schedule of payments (see Sub-Clause 14.4), with the Instructions to Tenderers specifying the criteria with which the Tenderer should comply. Since the Contractor would then have to arrange his own financing to cover the shortfall between the payments and his outgoings, he (and his financing bank) would probably require some form of security, guaranteeing payment when due.

It may be appropriate for the Employer, when preparing the tender documents, to anticipate the latter requirement by undertaking to provide a guarantee for the element of payment which the Contractor is to receive when the Works are complete. The acceptable form(s) of guarantee should be included in the tender documents, annexed to the Particular Conditions: an example form is annexed to this document, as Annex G. The following Sub-Clause may be added.

EXAMPLE PROVISIONS FOR CONTRACTOR FINANCE

The Employer shall obtain (at his cost) a payment guarantee in the amount and currencies, and provided by an entity, as stated in the Appendix to Tender. The Employer shall deliver the guarantee to the Contractor within 28 days after both Parties have entered into the Contract Agreement. The guarantee shall be in the form annexed to these Particular Conditions, or in another form acceptable to the Contractor. Unless and until the Contractor receives the guarantee, the Engineer shall not give the notice under Sub-Clause 8.1.

The guarantee shall be returned to the Employer at the earliest of the following dates:

(a) when the Contractor has been paid the Accepted Contract Amount;

(b) when obligations under the guarantee expire or have been discharged; or

(c) when the Employer has performed all obligations under the Contract.

Clause 15   Termination by Employer

Sub-Clause 15.2   Termination by Employer

Before inviting tenders, the Employer should verify that the wording of this Sub-Clause, and each anticipated ground for termination, is consistent with the law governing the Contract.

Sub-Clause 15.5   Employer's Entitlement to Termination

Unless inconsistent with the requirements of the Employer and/or financing institutions, a further sentence may be added.

EXAMPLE   Insert at the end of Sub-Clause 15.5:

The Employer shall also pay to the Contractor the amount of any other loss or damage resulting from this termination.

Clause 16   Suspension and Termination by Contractor

Sub-Clause 16.2   Termination by Contractor

Before inviting tenders, the Employer should verify that the wording of this Sub-Clause is consistent with the law governing the Contract. The Contractor should verify that each anticipated ground for termination is consistent with such law.

Clause 17   Risk and Responsibility

Sub-Clause 17.6   Limitation of Liability

EXAMPLE

In Sub-Clause 17.6, the sum referred to in the penultimate sentence shall be _____

Additional Sub-Clause   Use of Employer's Accommodation/Facilities

If the Contractor is to occupy the Employer's facilities temporarily, an additional sub-clause may be added:

EXAMPLE SUB-CLAUSE

The Contractor shall take full responsibility for the care of the items detailed below, from the respective dates of use or occupation by the Contractor, up to the respective dates of hand-over or cessation of occupation (where hand-over or cessation of occupation may take place after the date stated in the Taking-Over Certificate for the Works):

(insert details)

If any loss or damage happens to any of the above items while the Contractor is responsible for their care, arising from any cause whatsoever other than those for which the Employer is liable, the Contractor shall, at his own cost, rectify the loss or damage to the satisfaction of the Engineer.

Clause 18   Insurance

The wording in the General Conditions describes the insurances which are to be arranged by the "insuring Party", who is to be the Contractor unless otherwise stated in the Particular Conditions. Insurances so provided by the Contractor are to be consistent with the general terms agreed with the Employer. The Instructions to Tenderers may therefore require tenderers to provide details of the proposed terms.

If the Employer is to arrange any of the insurances under this Clause, the tender documents should include details as an annex to the Particular Conditions (so that tenderers can estimate what other insurances they wish to have for their own protection), including the conditions, limits, exceptions and deductibles; preferably in the form of a copy of each policy. The Employer may find it difficult to effect the insurances described in the third paragraph of Sub-Clause 18.2 (for Contractor's Equipment, which includes Subcontractor's equipment), because the Employer may not know the amount or value of these items of equipment. The following sentence may be included in the Particular Conditions:

EXAMPLE   Delete the final paragraph of Sub-Clause 18.2 and substitute:

However, the insurances described in the first two paragraphs of Sub-Clause 18.2 shall be effected and maintained by the Employer as insuring Party, and not by the Contractor.

Clause 19   Force Majeure

Before inviting tenders, the Employer should verify that the wording of this Clause is compatible with the law governing the Contract.

Clause 20   Claims, Disputes and Arbitration

Sub-Clause 20.2   Appointment of the Dispute Adjudication Board

Unless the Engineer (although appointed by the Employer) is to make the pre-arbitral decisions under this Clause 20, in accordance with the alternative option described below, the Contract should include the provisions under Clause 20 which, whilst not discouraging the Parties from reaching agreement on disputes as the works proceed, allow them to refer contentious matters to an impartial dispute adjudication board ("DAB").

The adjudication procedure depends for its success on, amongst other things, the Parties' confidence in the agreed individual(s) who will serve on the DAB. Therefore, it is essential that candidates for this position are not imposed by either Party on the other Party; and that, if the individual is selected under Sub-Clause 20.3, the selection is made by a wholly impartial entity. FIDIC is prepared to perform this role, if this authority has been delegated in accordance with the example wording in the Appendix to Tender.

It is preferable, but not essential, for the individual(s) to be agreed before the Letter of Acceptance is issued, and for the DAB to visit the Site on a regular basis. Under the example text in the Appendix to Tender, the Parties may either so agree before the Letter of Acceptance is issued or agree the appointment within the specified period thereafter. Alternatively, the Parties may prefer to defer the appointment until a dispute has arisen, in which case Sub-Clause 20.2 plus the Appendix - General Conditions of Dispute Adjudication Agreement with its Annex (Procedural Rules) and the Dispute Adjudication Agreement should be amended to comply with the wording contained in the corresponding sections of FIDIC's Conditions of Contract for Plant and Design - Build.

Sub-Clause 20.2 provides for two alternative arrangements for the DAB:

(a) one person, who acts as the sole member of the DAB, having entered into a tripartite agreement with both Parties; or

(b) a DAB of three persons, each of whom has entered into a tripartite agreement with both Parties.

The form of this tripartite agreement could be one of the two alternatives shown at the end of this publication, as appropriate to the arrangement adopted. Both of these forms incorporate (by reference) the General Conditions of Dispute Adjudication Agreement, which are included as the Appendix to the General Conditions because they are also referred to in Sub-Clause 20.2. Under either of these alternative forms of Dispute Adjudication Agreement, each individual person is referred to as a Member.

At an early stage, consideration should be given as to whether a one-person or three-person DAB is preferable for a particular project, taking account of its size, duration and the fields of expertise which will be involved. For some projects, it may be considered appropriate to appoint a one-person DAB for each major field of expertise relevant to the Works; however, this may give rise to problems if, when a dispute arises, the Parties cannot agree which field is applicable and, therefore, to whom the dispute should be referred.

For a one-person DAB to be mutually agreed, the Employer (or the tenderer) could propose the names and curriculum vitae of suitable persons, for the tenderer (or the Employer) to accept. It may be advisable to propose alternates in case some subsequently decline the appointment, assuming that they have not previously indicated their willingness to accept. Each Party may be reluctant to choose names from a list of people who have already been contacted by the other Party.

For a three-person DAB, the Employer and the tenderer may each propose one member, similar to the above procedure, for the tenderer and the Employer respectively to accept. For the chairman, the Employer (or the tenderer) could similarly propose suitable persons for the tenderer (or the Employer) to accept. It may be appropriate for the chairman's retainer fee to be more than that of the other two members, reflecting the additional administrative tasks which a chairman will have to perform.

The appointment of the DAB may be facilitated, especially if the members are not to be appointed at the commencement of the Contract, by including an agreed list of potential members in the Contract: in a Schedule.

Alternatively, the Engineer may make these pre-arbitral decisions. This alternative, which has been the Engineer's traditional role in common law countries, may be appropriate if the Engineer is an independent professional consulting engineer with the experience and resources required for the administration of all aspects of the contract. The Employer should recognise that, although the Engineer generally acts for the Employer as specified in Sub-Clause 3.1(a), the Engineer will make these pre-arbitral decisions impartially and the Employer must not prejudice this impartiality. If this alternative is considered appropriate, the Sub-Clause may be varied:

EXAMPLE SUB-CLAUSE FOR PRE-ARBITRAL DECISIONS BY THE ENGINEER

Delete Sub-Clauses 20.2 and 20.3.

Delete the second paragraph of Sub-Clause 20.4 and substitute:

The Engineer shall act as the DAB in accordance with this Sub-Clause 20.4, acting fairly, impartially and at the cost of the Employer. In the event that the Employer intends to replace the Engineer, the Employer's notice under Sub-Clause 3.4 shall include detailed proposals for the appointment of a replacement DAB.

Sub-Clause 20.5   Amicable Settlement

The provisions of this Sub-Clause are intended to encourage the parties to settle a dispute amicably, without the need for arbitration: for example, by direct negotiation, conciliation, mediation, or other forms of alternative dispute resolution. Amicable settlement procedures often depend, for their success, on confidentiality and on both Parties' acceptance of the procedure. Therefore, neither Party should seek to impose the procedure on the other Party.

Sub-Clause 20.6   Arbitration

The Contract should include provisions for the resolution by international arbitration of any disputes which are not resolved amicably. In international construction contracts, international commercial arbitration has numerous advantages over litigation in national courts, and may be more acceptable to the Parties.

Careful consideration should be given to ensuring that the international arbitration rules chosen are compatible with the provisions of Clause 20 and with the other elements to be set out in the Appendix to Tender. The Rules of Arbitration of the International Chamber of Commerce (the "ICC", which is based at 38 Cours Albert 1er, 75008 Paris, France) are frequently included in international contracts. In the absence of specific stipulations as to the number of arbitrators and the place of arbitration, the International Court of Arbitration of the ICC will decide on the number of arbitrators (typically three in any substantial construction dispute) and on the place of arbitration.

If the UNCITRAL (or other non-ICC) arbitration rules are preferred, it may be necessary to designate, in the Appendix to Tender, an institution to appoint the arbitrators or to administer the arbitration, unless the institution is named (and their role specified) in the arbitration rules. It may also be necessary to ensure, before so designating an institution in the Appendix to Tender, that it is prepared to appoint or administer.

For major projects tendered internationally, it is desirable that the place of arbitration be situated in a country other than that of the Employer or Contractor. This country should have a modern and liberal arbitration law and should have ratified a bilateral or multilateral convention (such as the 1958 New York Convention on the Recognition and Enforcement of Foreign Arbitral Awards), or both, that would facilitate the enforcement of an arbitral award in the states of the Parties.

It may be considered desirable in some cases for other Parties to be joined into any arbitration between the Parties, thereby creating a multi-party arbitration. While this may be feasible, multi-party arbitration clauses require skilful drafting, and usually need to be prepared on a case-by-case basis. No satisfactory standard form of multi-party arbitration clause for international use has yet been developed.

Annexes   FORMS OF SECURITIES

Acceptable form(s) of security should be included in the tender documents: for Annex A and/or B, in the Instructions to Tenderers; and for Annexes C to G, annexed to the Particular Conditions. The following example forms, which (except for Annex A) incorporate Uniform Rules published by the International Chamber of Commerce (the "ICC", which is based at 38 Cours Albert 1er, 75008 Paris, France), may have to be amended to comply with the applicable law. Although the ICC publishes guides to these Uniform Rules, legal advice should be taken before the securities are written. Note that the guaranteed amounts should be quoted in all the currencies, as specified in the Contract, in which the guarantor pays the beneficiary.

Annex A EXAMPLE FORM OF PARENT COMPANY GUARANTEE

[See page 3, and the comments on Sub-Clause 1.14]

Brief description of Contract _____

Name and address of Employer _____

_____ (together with successors and assigns).

We have been informed that _____ (hereinafter called the "Contractor") is submitting an offer for such Contract in response to your invitation, and that the conditions of your invitation require his offer to be supported by a parent company guarantee.

In consideration of you, the Employer, awarding the Contract to the Contractor, we (*name of parent company*) _____ irrevocably and unconditionally guarantee to you, as a primary obligation, the due performance of all the Contractor's obligations and liabilities under the Contract, including the Contractor's compliance with all its terms and conditions according to their true intent and meaning.

If the Contractor fails to so perform his obligations and liabilities and comply with the Contract, we will indemnify the Employer against and from all damages, losses and expenses (including legal fees and expenses) which arise from any such failure for which the Contractor is liable to the Employer under the Contract.

This guarantee shall come into full force and effect when the Contract comes into full force and effect. If the Contract does not come into full force and effect within a year of the date of this guarantee, or if you demonstrate that you do not intend to enter into the Contract with the Contractor, this guarantee shall be void and ineffective. This guarantee shall continue in full force and effect until all the Contractor's obligations and liabilities under the Contract have been discharged, when this guarantee shall expire and shall be returned to us, and our liability hereunder shall be discharged absolutely.

This guarantee shall apply and be supplemental to the Contract as amended or varied by the Employer and the Contractor from time to time. We hereby authorise them to agree any such amendment or variation, the due performance of which and compliance with which by the Contractor are likewise guaranteed hereunder. Our obligations and liabilities under this guarantee shall not be discharged by any allowance of time or other indulgence whatsoever by the Employer to the Contractor, or by any variation or suspension of the works to be executed under the Contract, or by any amendments to the Contract or to the constitution of the Contractor or the Employer, or by any other matters, whether with or without our knowledge or consent.

This guarantee shall be governed by the law of the same country (or other jurisdiction) as that which governs the Contract and any dispute under this guarantee shall be finally settled under the Rules of Arbitration of the International Chamber of Commerce by one or more arbitrators appointed in accordance with such Rules. We confirm that the benefit of this guarantee may be assigned subject only to the provisions for assignment of the Contract.

Date _____ Signature(s) _____

Annex B   EXAMPLE FORM OF TENDER SECURITY

[See page 3]

Brief description of Contract ....

Name and address of Beneficiary ....

.... (whom the tender documents define as the Employer).

We have been informed that .... (hereinafter called the "Principal") is submitting an offer for such Contract in response to your invitation, and that the conditions of your invitation (the "conditions of invitation", which are set out in a document entitled Instructions to Tenderers) require his offer to be supported by a tender security.

At the request of the Principal, we (*name of bank*) .... hereby irrevocably undertake to pay you, the Beneficiary/Employer, any sum or sums not exceeding in total the amount of .... (say: ....) upon receipt by us of your demand in writing and your written statement (in the demand) stating that:

(a)   the Principal has, without your agreement, withdrawn his offer after the latest time specified for its submission and before the expiry of its period of validity, or

(b)   the Principal has refused to accept the correction of errors in his offer in accordance with such conditions of invitation, or

(c)   you awarded the Contract to the Principal and he has failed to comply with sub-clause 1.6 of the conditions of the Contract, or

(d)   you awarded the Contract to the Principal and he has failed to comply with sub-clause 4.2 of the conditions of the Contract.

Any demand for payment must contain your signature(s) which must be authenticated by your bankers or by a notary public. The authenticated demand and statement must be received by us at this office on or before (*the date 35 days after the expiry of the validity of the Letter of Tender*) .... , when this guarantee shall expire and shall be returned to us.

This guarantee is subject to the Uniform Rules for Demand Guarantees, published as number 458 by the International Chamber of Commerce, except as stated above.

Date .... Signature(s) ....

Annex C   EXAMPLE FORM OF PERFORMANCE SECURITY - DEMAND GUARANTEE

[See comments on Sub-Clause 4.2]

Brief description of Contract _____

Name and address of Beneficiary _____

_____ (whom the Contract defines as the Employer).

We have been informed that _____ (hereinafter called the "Principal") is your contractor under such Contract, which requires him to obtain a performance security.

At the request of the Principal, we (*name of bank*) _____ hereby irrevocably undertake to pay you, the Beneficiary/Employer, any sum or sums not exceeding in total the amount of _____ (the "guaranteed amount", say: _____) upon receipt by us of your demand in writing and your written statement stating:

(a)   that the Principal is in breach of his obligation(s) under the Contract, and

(b)   the respect in which the Principal is in breach.

[Following the receipt by us of an authenticated copy of the taking-over certificate for the whole of the works under clause 10 of the conditions of the Contract, such guaranteed amount shall be reduced by _____ % and we shall promptly notify you that we have received such certificate and have reduced the guaranteed amount accordingly.] [1]

Any demand for payment must contain your [minister's/directors'] [1] signature(s) which must be authenticated by your bankers or by a notary public. The authenticated demand and statement must be received by us at this office on or before (*the date 70 days after the expected expiry of the Defects Notification Period for the Works*) _____ (the "expiry date"), when this guarantee shall expire and shall be returned to us.

We have been informed that the Beneficiary may require the Principal to extend this guarantee if the performance certificate under the Contract has not been issued by the date 28 days prior to such expiry date. We undertake to pay you such guaranteed amount upon receipt by us, within such period of 28 days, of your demand in writing and your written statement that the performance certificate has not been issued, for reasons attributable to the Principal, and that this guarantee has not been extended.

This guarantee shall be governed by the laws of _____ and shall be subject to the Uniform Rules for Demand Guarantees, published as number 458 by the International Chamber of Commerce, except as stated above.

Date _____   Signature(s) _____

---

[1] *When writing the tender documents, the writer should ascertain whether to include the optional text, shown in parentheses [ ]*

Annex D   EXAMPLE FORM OF PERFORMANCE SECURITY - SURETY BOND

[See comments on Sub-Clause 4.2]

Brief description of Contract _____

Name and address of Beneficiary _____

_____ (together with successors and assigns, all as defined in the Contract as the Employer).

By this Bond, (*name and address of contractor*) _____
(who is the contractor under such Contract) as Principal and (*name and address of guarantor*) _____ as Guarantor are irrevocably held and firmly bound to the Beneficiary in the total amount of _____ (the "Bond Amount", say: _____) for the due performance of all such Principal's obligations and liabilities under the Contract. [Such Bond Amount shall be reduced by ____ % upon the issue of the taking-over certificate for the whole of the works under clause 10 of the conditions of the Contract.][1]

This Bond shall become effective on the Commencement Date defined in the Contract.

Upon Default by the Principal to perform any Contractual Obligation, or upon the occurrence of any of the events and circumstances listed in sub-clause 15.2 of the conditions of the Contract, the Guarantor shall satisfy and discharge the damages sustained by the Beneficiary due to such Default, event or circumstances.[2] However, the total liability of the Guarantor shall not exceed the Bond Amount.

The obligations and liabilities of the Guarantor shall not be discharged by any allowance of time or other indulgence whatsoever by the Beneficiary to the Principal, or by any variation or suspension of the works to be executed under the Contract, or by any amendments to the Contract or to the constitution of the Principal or the Beneficiary, or by any other matters, whether with or without the knowledge or consent of the Guarantor.

Any claim under this Bond must be received by the Guarantor on or before (*the date six months after the expected expiry of the Defects Notification Period for the Works*) _____ (the "Expiry Date"), when this Bond shall expire and shall be returned to the Guarantor.

The benefit of this Bond may be assigned subject to the provisions for assignment of the Contract, and subject to the receipt by the Guarantor of evidence of full compliance with such provisions.

This Bond shall be governed by the law of the same country (or other jurisdiction) as that which governs the Contract. This Bond incorporates and shall be subject to the Uniform Rules for Contract Bonds, published as number 524 by the International Chamber of Commerce, and words used in this Bond shall bear the meanings set out in such Rules.

Wherefore this Bond has been issued by the Principal and the Guarantor on (*date*) _____

Signature(s) for and on behalf of the Principal _____

Signature(s) for and on behalf of the Guarantor _____

[1] *When writing the tender documents, the writer should ascertain whether to include the optional text, shown in parentheses* [ ]
[2] *Insert:* [and shall not be entitled to perform the Principal's obligations under the Contract.]
     Or: [or at the option of the Guarantor (to be exercised in writing within 42 days of receiving the claim specifying such Default) perform the Principal's obligations under the Contract.]

Annex E   EXAMPLE FORM OF ADVANCE PAYMENT GUARANTEE

[See comments on Sub-Clause 14.2]

Brief description of Contract _____

Name and address of Beneficiary _____

_____ (whom the Contract defines as the Employer).

We have been informed that _____ (hereinafter called the "Principal") is your contractor under such Contract and wishes to receive an advance payment, for which the Contract requires him to obtain a guarantee.

At the request of the Principal, we (*name of bank*) _____ hereby irrevocably undertake to pay you, the Beneficiary/Employer, any sum or sums not exceeding in total the amount of _____ (the "guaranteed amount", say: _____) upon receipt by us of your demand in writing and your written statement stating:

(a)   that the Principal has failed to repay the advance payment in accordance with the conditions of the Contract, and

(b)   the amount which the Principal has failed to repay.

This guarantee shall become effective upon receipt [of the first instalment] of the advance payment by the Principal. Such guaranteed amount shall be reduced by the amounts of the advance payment repaid to you, as evidenced by your notices issued under sub-clause 14.6 of the conditions of the Contract. Following receipt (from the Principal) of a copy of each purported notice, we shall promptly notify you of the revised guaranteed amount accordingly.

Any demand for payment must contain your signature(s) which must be authenticated by your bankers or by a notary public. The authenticated demand and statement must be received by us at this office on or before (*the date 70 days after the expected expiry of the Time for Completion*) _____ (the "expiry date"), when this guarantee shall expire and shall be returned to us.

We have been informed that the Beneficiary may require the Principal to extend this guarantee if the advance payment has not been repaid by the date 28 days prior to such expiry date. We undertake to pay you such guaranteed amount upon receipt by us, within such period of 28 days, of your demand in writing and your written statement that the advance payment has not been repaid and that this guarantee has not been extended.

This guarantee shall be governed by the laws of _____ and shall be subject to the Uniform Rules for Demand Guarantees, published as number 458 by the International Chamber of Commerce, except as stated above.

Date _____   Signature(s) _____

Annex F   EXAMPLE FORM OF RETENTION MONEY GUARANTEE

[See comments on Sub-Clause 14.9]

Brief description of Contract _____

Name and address of Beneficiary _____ _____

_____ (whom the Contract defines as the Employer).

We have been informed that _____ (hereinafter called the "Principal") is your contractor under such Contract and wishes to receive early payment of [part of] the retention money, for which the Contract requires him to obtain a guarantee.

At the request of the Principal, we (*name of bank*) _____ hereby irrevocably undertake to pay you, the Beneficiary/Employer, any sum or sums not exceeding in total the amount of _____ (the "guaranteed amount", say: _____) upon receipt by us of your demand in writing and your written statement stating:

(a)   that the Principal has failed to carry out his obligation(s) to rectify certain defect(s) for which he is responsible under the Contract, and

(b)   the nature of such defect(s).

At any time, our liability under this guarantee shall not exceed the total amount of retention money released to the Principal by you, as evidenced by your notices issued under sub-clause 14.6 of the conditions of the Contract with a copy being passed to us.

Any demand for payment must contain your signature(s) which must be authenticated by your bankers or by a notary public. The authenticated demand and statement must be received by us at this office on or before (*the date 70 days after the expected expiry of the Defects Notification Period for the Works*) _____ (the "expiry date"), when this guarantee shall expire and shall be returned to us.

We have been informed that the Beneficiary may require the Principal to extend this guarantee if the performance certificate under the Contract has not been issued by the date 28 days prior to such expiry date. We undertake to pay you such guaranteed amount upon receipt by us, within such period of 28 days, of your demand in writing and your written statement that the performance certificate has not been issued, for reasons attributable to the Principal, and that this guarantee has not been extended.

This guarantee shall be governed by the laws of _____ and shall be subject to the Uniform Rules for Demand Guarantees, published as number 458 by the International Chamber of Commerce, except as stated above.

Date _____   Signature(s) _____

Annex G   EXAMPLE FORM OF PAYMENT GUARANTEE BY EMPLOYER

[See page 17: Contractor Finance]

Brief description of Contract _____

Name and address of Beneficiary _____

_____ (whom the Contract defines as the Contractor).

We have been informed that _____ (whom the Contract defines as the Employer and who is hereinafter called the "Principal") is required to obtain a bank guarantee.

At the request of the Principal, we (*name of bank*) _____ hereby irrevocably undertake to pay you, the Beneficiary/Contractor, any sum or sums not exceeding in total the amount of _____ (say: _____) upon receipt by us of your demand in writing and your written statement stating:

(a)   that, in respect of a payment due under the Contract, the Principal has failed to make payment in full by the date fourteen days after the expiry of the period specified in the Contract as that within which such payment should have been made, and

(b)   the amount(s) which the Principal has failed to pay.

Any demand for payment must be accompanied by a copy of [*list of documents evidencing entitlement to payment*] _____ , in respect of which the Principal has failed to make payment in full.

Any demand for payment must contain your signature(s) which must be authenticated by your bankers or by a notary public. The authenticated demand and statement must be received by us at this office on or before (*the date six months after the expected expiry of the Defects Notification Period for the Works*) _____ when this guarantee shall expire and shall be returned to us.

This guarantee shall be governed by the laws of _____ and shall be subject to the Uniform Rules for Demand Guarantees, published as number 458 by the International Chamber of Commerce, except as stated above.

Date _____   Signature(s) _____

GENERAL CONDITIONS

GUIDANCE FOR THE
PREPARATION OF
PARTICULAR CONDITIONS

FORMS OF LETTER OF
TENDER, CONTRACT
AGREEMENT AND
DISPUTE ADJUDICATION
AGREEMENT

Conditions of Contract
for CONSTRUCTION

FOR BUILDING AND ENGINEERING WORKS DESIGNED BY THE EMPLOYER

Forms of Letter of Tender, Contract Agreement
and Dispute Adjudication Agreement

FEDERATION INTERNATIONALE DES INGENIEURS-CONSEILS
INTERNATIONAL FEDERATION OF CONSULTING ENGINEERS
INTERNATIONALE VEREINIGUNG BERATENDER INGENIEURE
FEDERACION INTERNACIONAL DE INGENIEROS CONSULTORES

FIDIC

LETTER OF TENDER

NAME OF CONTRACT:

TO:

We have examined the Conditions of Contract, Specification, Drawings, Bill of Quantities, the other Schedules, the attached Appendix and Addenda Nos _____ for the execution of the above-named Works. We offer to execute and complete the Works and remedy any defects therein in conformity with this Tender which includes all these documents, for the sum of (in currencies of payment) _____

_____

or such other sum as may be determined in accordance with the Conditions of Contract.
We accept your suggestions for the appointment of the DAB, as set out in Schedule _____

> [*We have completed the Schedule by adding our suggestions for the other Member of the DAB, but these suggestions are not conditions of this offer*].*

We agree to abide by this Tender until _____ and it shall remain binding upon us and may be accepted at any time before that date. We acknowledge that the Appendix forms part of this Letter of Tender.

If this offer is accepted, we will provide the specified Performance Security, commence the Works as soon as is reasonably practicable after the Commencement Date, and complete the Works in accordance with the above-named documents within the Time for Completion.

Unless and until a formal Agreement is prepared and executed this Letter of Tender, together with your written acceptance thereof, shall constitute a binding contract between us.

We understand that you are not bound to accept the lowest or any tender you may receive.

Signature _____ in the capacity of _____

duly authorised to sign tenders for and on behalf of _____

_____

Address: _____

_____

Date: _____

* If the Tenderer does not accept, this paragraph may be deleted and replaced by:

> We do not accept your suggestions for the appointment of the DAB. We have included our suggestions in the Schedule, but these suggestions are not conditions of this offer. If these suggestions are not acceptable to you, we propose that the DAB be jointly appointed in accordance with Sub-Clause 20.2 of the Conditions of Contract.

i

APPENDIX TO TENDER

[Note: with the exception of the items for which the Employer's requirements have been inserted, the following information must be completed before the Tender is submitted]

Item	Sub-Clause	Data
Employer's name and address	1.1.2.2 & 1.3.	
Contractor's name and address	1.1.2.3 & 1.3.	
Engineer's name and address	1.1.2.4 & 1.3.	
Time for Completion of the Works	1.1.3.3	____ days
Defects Notification Period	1.1.3.7	365 days
Electronic transmission systems	1.3	
Governing Law	1.4	
Ruling language	1.4	
Language for communications	1.4	
Time for access to the Site	2.1	____ days after Commencement Date
Amount of Performance Security	4.2	_____ % of the Accepted Contract Amount, in the currencies and proportions in which the Contract Price is payable
Normal working hours	6.5	
Delay damages for the Works	8.7 & 14.15(b)	____ % of the final Contract Price per day, in the currencies and proportions in which the Contract Price is payable
Maximum amount of delay damages . .	8.7	_____ % of the final Contract Price
If there are Provisional Sums: Percentage for adjustment of Provisional Sums	13.5(b)	_____ %

Initials of signatory of Tender _____

If Sub-Clause 13.8 applies:
　Adjustments for Changes in Cost;
　Table(s) of adjustment data . . . .　13.8 . . . .　for payments each
　　　　　　　　　　　　　　　　　　　　　month/[*YEAR*] in _____ (*currency*)

Coefficient; scope of index	Country of origin; currency of index	Source of index; Title/definition	Value on stated date(s)* Value	Date
a= 0.10　Fixed				
b= ____　Labour				
c=				
d=				
e=				

* These values and dates confirm the definition of each index, but do not define Base Date indices

Total advance payment . . . .　14.2 . . . .　____ % of the Accepted Contract Amount

Number and timing of instalments . . . .　14.2 . . . .　_____

Currencies and proportions . . . .　14.2 . . . .　____ % in _____
　　　　　　　　　　　　　　　　　　　　　____ % in _____

Start repayment of advance payment .　14.2(a)　when payments are _____ %
　　　　　　　　　　　　　　　　　　　　　of the Accepted Contract Amount less Provisional Sums

Repayment amortisation of advance
payment . . . .　14.2(b) . . . . .　____ %

Percentage of retention . . . .　14.3 . . . .　____ %

Limit of Retention Money . . . .　14.3 . . . .　____ % of the Accepted Contract Amount

If Sub-Clause 14.5 applies:
　Plant and Materials for payment
　when shipped en route to the Site . .　14.5(b) . . . . .　_____ [list]
　　　　　　　　　　　　　　　　　　　　　_____ [list]

　Plant and Materials for payment
　when delivered to the Site . . . .　14.5(c) . . . . .　_____ [list]
　　　　　　　　　　　　　　　　　　　　　_____ [list]

Minimum amount of Interim Payment
Certificates . . . .　14.6 . . . .　____ % of the Accepted Contract Amount

If payments are only to be made in a currency/currencies named on the first page of the Letter of Tender:

　Currency/currencies of payment . . . .　14.15 . . . . . .　as named in the Letters of Tender

Initials of signatory of Tender　_____

If some payments are to be made in a currency/currencies not named on the first page of the Letter of Tender:

Currencies of payment 14.15

Currency Unit	Percentage payable in the Currency	Rate of exchange: number of Local per unit of Foreign
Local: [name]		1.000
Foreign: [name]		
[name]		

Periods for submission of insurance:

(a) evidence of insurance	18.1		____ days
(b) relevant policies	18.1		____ days

Maximum amount of deductibles for
insurance of the Employer's risks . . . .   18.2(d) . . . . .

Minimum amount of third party
insurance . . . .   18.3 . . . .

Date by which the DAB shall be appointed .   20.2 . . . .   28 days after the Commencement Date

The DAB shall be . . . .   20.2 . . . .   *Either:*
   _____ One sole Member/adjudicator
   Or:
   _____ A DAB of three Members

Appointment (if not agreed) to be
made by . . . .   20.3 . . . .   The President of FIDIC or a person appointed by the President

If there are Sections:
   Definition of Sections:

Description (Sub-Clause 1.1.5.6)	Time for Completion (Sub-Clause 1.1.3.3)	Delay Damages (Sub-Clause 8.7)

[In the above Appendix, the text shown in italics is intended to assist the drafter of a particular contract by providing guidance on which provisions are relevant to the particular contract. This italicised text should not be included in the tender documents, as it will generally appear inappropriate to tenderers.]

Initials of signatory of Tender _____

CONTRACT AGREEMENT

This Agreement made the _____ day of _____ 20 _____

Between _____ of _____ (hereinafter called "the Employer") of the one part,
and _____ of _____ (hereinafter called "the Contractor") of the other part

Whereas the Employer desires that the Works known as _____ should be executed by the Contractor, and has accepted a Tender by the Contractor for the execution and completion of these Works and the remedying of any defects therein,

The Employer and the Contractor agree as follows:

1.   In this Agreement words and expressions shall have the same meanings as are respectively assigned to them in the Conditions of Contract hereinafter referred to.

2.   The following documents shall be deemed to form and be read and construed as part of this Agreement:

      (a)   The Letter of Acceptance dated _____

      (b)   The Letter of Tender dated _____

      (c)   The Addenda nos. _____

      (d)   The Conditions of Contract

      (e)   The Specification

      (f)   The Drawings, and

      (g)   The completed Schedules.

3.   In consideration of the payments to be made by the Employer to the Contractor as hereinafter mentioned, the Contractor hereby covenants with the Employer to execute and complete the Works and remedy any defects therein, in conformity with the provisions of the Contract.

4.   The Employer hereby covenants to pay the Contractor, in consideration of the execution and completion of the Works and the remedying of defects therein, the Contract Price at the times and in the manner prescribed by the Contract.

In Witness whereof the parties hereto have caused this Agreement to be executed the day and year first before written in accordance with their respective laws.

SIGNED by: _____   SIGNED by: _____

for and on behalf of the Employer in the presence of

for and on behalf of the Contractor in the presence of

Witness: _____   Witness: _____
Name: _____   Name: _____
Address: _____   Address: _____
Date: _____   Date: _____

V

DISPUTE ADJUDICATION AGREEMENT

[for a one-person DAB]

Name and details of Contract
Name and address of Employer
Name and address of Contractor
Name and address of Member

Whereas the Employer and the Contractor have entered into the Contract and desire jointly to appoint the Member to act as sole adjudicator who is also called the "DAB".

The Employer, Contractor and Member jointly agree as follows:

1.　The conditions of this Dispute Adjudication Agreement comprise the "General Conditions of Dispute Adjudication Agreement", which is appended to the General Conditions of the "Conditions of Contract for Construction" First Edition 1999 published by the Fédération Internationale des Ingénieurs-Conseils (FIDIC), and the following provisions. In these provisions, which include amendments and additions to the General Conditions of Dispute Adjudication Agreement, words and expressions shall have the same meanings as are assigned to them in the General Conditions of Dispute Adjudication Agreement.

2.　[*Details of amendments to the General Conditions of Dispute Adjudication Agreement, if any. For example:*

In the procedural rules annexed to the General Conditions of Dispute Adjudication Agreement, Rule _ is deleted and replaced by: " ... "]

3.　In accordance with Clause 6 of the General Conditions of Dispute Adjudication Agreement, the Member shall be paid as follows:

A retainer fee of _____ per calendar month,
plus a daily fee of _____ per day.

4.　In consideration of these fees and other payments to be made by the Employer and the Contractor in accordance with Clause 6 of the General Conditions of Dispute Adjudication Agreement, the Member undertakes to act as the DAB (as adjudicator) in accordance with this Dispute Adjudication Agreement.

5.　The Employer and the Contractor jointly and severally undertake to pay the Member, in consideration of the carrying out of these services, in accordance with Clause 6 of the General Conditions of Dispute Adjudication Agreement.

6.　This Dispute Adjudication Agreement shall be governed by the law of _____

SIGNED by: _____　　SIGNED by: _____　　SIGNED by: _____

for and on behalf of the Employer　for and on behalf of the Contractor　the Member in the presence of
in the presence of　　　　　　in the presence of

Witness: _____　　Witness: _____　　Witness _____
Name: _____　　Name: _____　　Name: _____
Address: _____　　Address: _____　　Address: _____
Date: _____　　Date: _____　　Date: _____

DISPUTE ADJUDICATION AGREEMENT

[for each member of a three-person DAB]

Name and details of Contract _____ _____
Name and address of Employer _____
Name and address of Contractor _____
Name and address of Member _____

Whereas the Employer and the Contractor have entered into the Contract and desire jointly to appoint the Member to act as one of the three persons who are jointly called the "DAB" *[and desire the Member to act as chairman of the DAB]*.

The Employer, Contractor and Member jointly agree as follows:

1. The conditions of this Dispute Adjudication Agreement comprise the "General Conditions of Dispute Adjudication Agreement", which is appended to the General Conditions of the "Conditions of Contract for Construction" First Edition 1999 published by the Fédération Internationale des Ingénieurs-Conseils (FIDIC), and the following provisions. In these provisions, which include amendments and additions to the General Conditions of Dispute Adjudication Agreement, words and expressions shall have the same meanings as are assigned to them in the General Conditions of Dispute Adjudication Agreement.

2. [*Details of amendments to the General Conditions of Dispute Adjudication Agreement, if any. For example:*

    In the procedural rules annexed to the General Conditions of Dispute Adjudication Agreement, Rule _ is deleted and replaced by: " ... "]

3. In accordance with Clause 6 of the General Conditions of Dispute Adjudication Agreement, the Member shall be paid as follows:

    > A retainer fee of _____ per calendar month,
    > plus a daily fee of _____ per day.

4. In consideration of these fees and other payments to be made by the Employer and the Contractor in accordance with Clause 6 of the General Conditions of Dispute Adjudication Agreement, the Member undertakes to serve, as described in this Dispute Adjudication Agreement, as one of the three persons who are jointly to act as the DAB.

5. The Employer and the Contractor jointly and severally undertake to pay the Member, in consideration of the carrying out of these services, in accordance with Clause 6 of the General Conditions of Dispute Adjudication Agreement.

6. This Dispute Adjudication Agreement shall be governed by the law of _____

SIGNED by: _____ SIGNED by: _____ SIGNED by: _____

for and on behalf of the Employer   for and on behalf of the Contractor   the Member in the presence of
in the presence of   in the presence of

Witness: _____ Witness: _____ Witness _____
Name: _____ Name: _____ Name: _____
Address: _____ Address: _____ Address: _____
Date: _____ Date: _____ Date: _____